THE ENCYCLOPEDIA OF
DOLLHOUSE-DECORATING
TECHNIQUES

THE ENCYCLOPEDIA OF
DOLLHOUSE-DECORATING
TECHNIQUES

William Davis • Caroline List • Nick Forder

RUNNING PRESS
PHILADELPHIA • LONDON

A QUARTO BOOK

Copyright © 1997 Quarto Inc

9 8 7 6 5 4 3 2 1

Digit on the right indicates the number of this printing

ISBN 0–7624–0095–1

Library of Congress Cataloguing-in-Publication Number
96–71944

This book was designed and produced by
Quarto Publishing plc
The Old Brewery
6 Blundell Street
London N7 9BH

Senior editor Kate Kirby
Senior art editor Catherine Shearman
Designer Julie Francis
Editor Cathy Meeus
Photographers Martin Norris, Richard Gleed
Picture researcher Zoe Holtermann
Art director Moira Clinch
Quarto would like to thank and acknowledge Dijon Ltd and Blackwells of
Hawkwell for supplying materials, fixtures and fittings for photography.

Typeset by Central Southern Typesetters, Eastbourne
Manufactured in Singapore by
Pica Colour Separations Overseas Pte Ltd
Printed in Singapore by Star Standard Ltd

This book may be ordered by mail from the publisher.
Please include $2.50 for postage and handling.
But try your bookstore first!
Running Press Book Publishers
125 South Twenty-second Street
Philadelphia, Pennsylvania 19103–4399

Foreword

Dollhouse making and miniature collecting have an ever-increasing following, with stores specializing in the supply of houses, furniture, and accessories opening in many towns and cities. The fascination with dollhouses is not confined simply to collecting ready-made items to furnish and decorate store-bought houses. Many contemporary enthusiasts derive much enjoyment from the skill and creativity that can be put into styling and decorating your own miniature homes. This may be in part due to the relatively high cost of well-designed finished dollhouses, but also surely owes much to the satisfaction to be gained from the craft of dollhouse decorating.

This book explains all you need to know to decorate and finish your dollhouse to a high standard: from preparing the surfaces and correcting imperfections in construction, to exterior and interior painting and wallpapering, through to the finishing touches. The information provided will enable even a newcomer to these skills to achieve excellent results. The step-by-step instructions show you how to plan each operation, tell you what tools and materials you will need, and give helpful tips of the trade wherever applicable. In many instances, techniques for making your own cost-saving materials have been described. The final section of the book contains a gallery of finished projects intended to provide ideas and inspiration.

The book is divided into sections for ease of reference, but I recommend that you read it all the way through before you start to work on your dollhouse, and then refer to the relevant sections as you proceed. I hope that with the help of this book you will succeed in creating your own distinctively decorated dollhouse that will provide hours of satisfaction for you as the work progresses and years of pleasure for you and your family once it is complete.

WILLIAM DAVIS

Contents

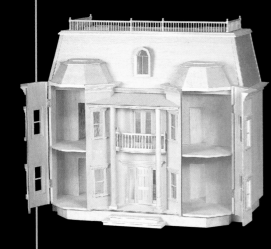

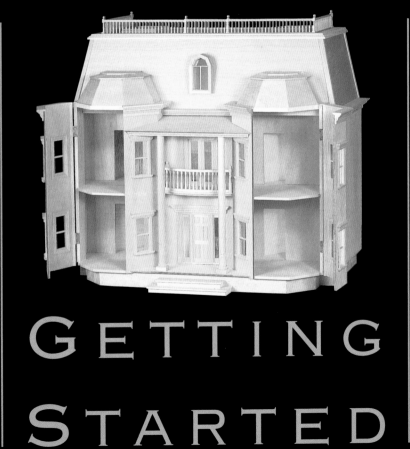

GETTING
STARTED

Planning

FOR MOST PEOPLE, THE STARTING POINT FOR DOLLHOUSE DECORATION IS THE HOUSE ITSELF. YOU MAY HAVE AN OLD DOLLHOUSE IN NEED OF REFURBISHMENT, OR YOU MAY HAVE BOUGHT OR PLAN TO BUY A READY-MADE HOUSE. DOLLHOUSE KITS, WHICH PROVIDE PRECUT WALLS, FLOORS, AND ROOF, ARE ANOTHER POPULAR OPTION FOR THOSE WHO DO NOT HAVE THE TIME OR THE SKILLS TO MAKE THEIR OWN HOUSE FROM SCRATCH. THESE KITS ARE THE PERFECT START FOR THE NEWCOMER TO THE WORLD OF DOLLHOUSE DECORATION.

A set of blank walls is the basis from which you can create houses as different as a Victorian town house, a clapboard farmhouse, or a Palladian mansion. The decorative techniques explained in this book open up a vast range of possibilities. Although most people choose to create a miniature home for their dollhouse, there are other options. It could be great fun to create an old-fashioned general store, with wooden counters and shelves, or you might prefer to make a miniature medieval castle, complete with flagstone floors and tapestries on the walls.

Even if you are not skilled in woodworking or other craft techniques, you can achieve a wide variety of decorative effects by taking advantage of the many products and accessories that are available from most dollhouse suppliers and modelmaking stores. The ideas for decorating exteriors and interiors that are described here cater for those of every level of expertise and can be adapted to meet individual requirements as you gain more experience. With care and patience you will create a unique finished dollhouse that will give you tremendous pleasure.

WORKING TO SCALE Success in the art of dollhouse decoration depends to a large extent on accurately translating life-sized features into the reduced scale of the world of the dollhouse. The most common scale used by manufacturers of quality dollhouses, furnishings, and accessories is 1:12. This means that the dollhouse items are one twelfth of the size of the real objects – for example, a 6-foot long dining table would be reduced to 6 inches in length. This is the scale used in the projects in this book. Having established your scale, it is important to stick to it as consistently as possible or the overall impact of the interior will suffer.

IDEAS FOR STYLE AND DECORATION For many dollhouse enthusiasts, a large part of the pleasure is derived from insuring the authenticity of the decoration and furnishings in their dollhouses. However, unless you happen to be an expert in architectural and design history, you will need to do careful research to make sure your choices look "right."

◀ The exterior of this Georgian-style townhouse is given character and authenticity through careful attention to details such as the pillared portico and "iron" railings.

◀ The impact of this superb miniature reconstruction of an early 19th century dining room owes a great deal to the fact that every detail has been rendered perfectly to scale.

▶ This country kitchen has provided the opportunity to use a number of interesting techniques, including imitation stone and brickwork.

▲ This atmospheric Victorian gentleman's study illustrates how simple decorative techniques and thoughtful selection of period accessories can create interiors of distinction.

Even if historic accuracy is not your chief concern, research into different styles can give you a wealth of ideas and inspiration to create original interiors of your own design.

You can learn a great deal by visiting museums and historic houses. Historic interiors depicted in old paintings are also a valuable source of inspiration, as are photographs, tourist guides and books on design history. But it is also important not to underestimate the value of your own observations. Take photographs or make sketches of houses' exteriors or room schemes that you encounter which have features that you might wish to reproduce in a dollhouse setting. Note details such as the type of flooring or the style of window frame. The colors used for walls or the fabrics used for drapes and furnishings are all an integral part of the period "feel" of an interior.

ORDER OF WORK

The order of work varies according to the type of project that you are undertaking. Always follow the instructions for the specific technique on which you are working, but the following advice applies in the majority of cases.

❶ Paint window frames, doors and door frames, staircases, baseboards, moldings, etc., before mounting them in place on the façade or in a room. Do not paint surfaces that are to be glued.

❷ Paint the exterior walls and roof next, and complete any necessary filling and sanding before starting work on the interior. You can then cover inadvertent paint splashes and clean up any dust produced by sanding before you start work on the more delicate interior decoration.

❸ When you start the interior decoration, begin with the ceilings. Brilliant white latex paint (silk finish) is the best choice since it reflects the maximum light into your room settings. If you plan to install coving or cornices on the ceiling, leave a gap unpainted around the edge of the ceiling so that the glue will stick securely. You can reserve the edges by covering them with narrow masking tape before you start painting.

❹ If the walls are to be painted, do this next. Leave the bottom edge of the walls bare if you want to put in baseboards.

❺ Apply the finish to the flooring.

❻ Finally, complete any final touches including wallpaper, doors, windows, baseboards, pillars, etc.

Tools and equipment

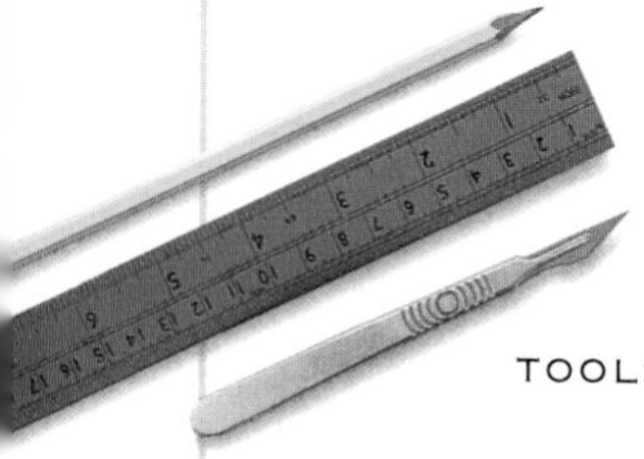

MOST OF THE TECHNIQUES IN THIS BOOK REQUIRE ONLY BASIC TOOLS AND EQUIPMENT. THE ITEMS SHOWN HERE AND OVERLEAF ARE NEEDED FOR MANY OF THE PROJECTS AND MAKE UP A BASIC STARTER KIT.

As you undertake more complex projects, you will gradually accumulate more equipment, although not necessarily at great expense. You will also find many different uses for your tools – for example, a good steel ruler serves both as a measure and as a first-rate cutting edge. Always check the tools and materials list given for each project before you start.

CHOOSING AND CARING FOR TOOLS When buying tools, it is a good rule always to buy the best quality you can afford. A good tool usually does the job better and will often last a lifetime. Look after your tools by keeping them well-ordered in a dry place. Change blades regularly. A sharp tool gives better results and is paradoxically often safer than a blunt one, which is more liable to slip.

❶ Tenon saw for cutting lengths of wood.

❷ Razor saw with standard and fine blades for cutting details.

❸ Miter block for straight and angled cuts.

❹ Junior hacksaw for cutting slates and tiles.

❺ Hard printer's roller for applying thin coats of paint.

❻ Modeling tools for marking wet putty.

❼ Fine-tooth file for smoothing rough edges.

❽ Long-nosed pliers for getting into corners.

❾ Lightweight hammer for punching in nails.

❿ Pin push for punching in nails in small spaces.

⓫ Awl for making holes.

⓬ Craft knife and scapel with spare blades.

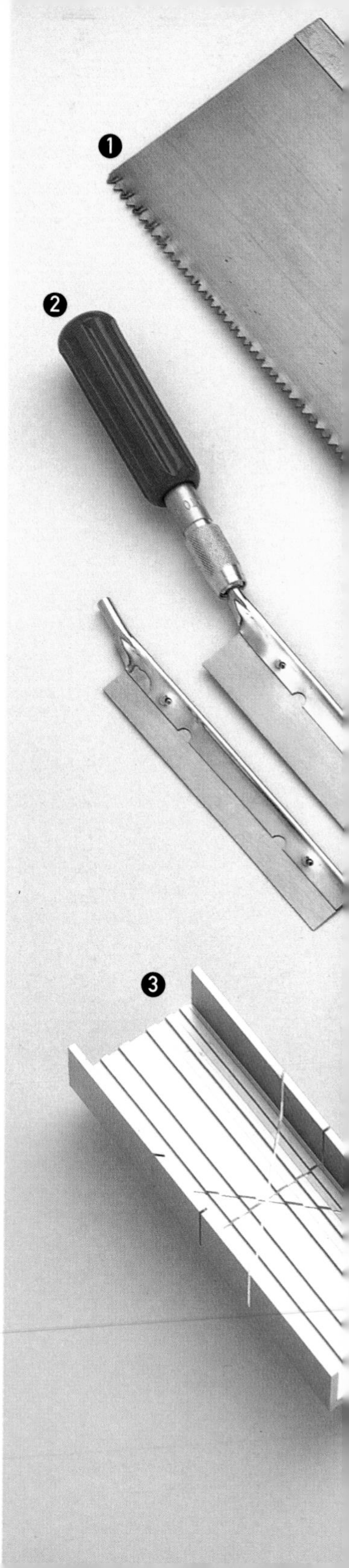

SAFETY

Always use your tools correctly and safely and remember the following safety guidelines.

• Wear protective goggles and a face mask when drilling, cutting, sawing, or sandpapering to prevent particles of sawdust from getting into your eyes and lungs.

• Choose nontoxic paint products and fungicide-free wallpaper paste whenever possible, especially if the dollhouse is intended for a child.

• Always wash your hands thoroughly with soap and water after working with paint, glue, putty, or paste to avoid the risk of ingesting toxic chemicals.

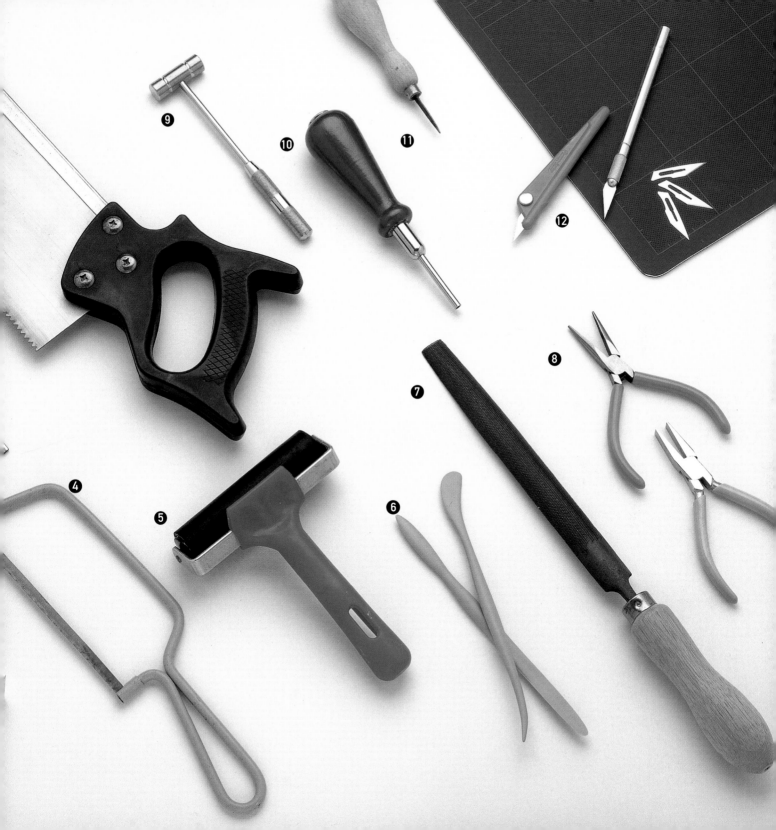

1 Masking tape to give clean edges.

2 Toothpicks for marking in wet putty.

3 Sponge for special paint effects.

4 Scraps for testing stains and varnishes.

5 Pencils for marking.

6 Eraser for correcting.

7 Scissors for cutting.

8 Spatula for spreading putty or glue.

9 Clean rags for removing excess glue.

10 Nail brush for stippling large areas.

11 Steel ruler for measuring.

12 White craft glue and multipurpose glue.

13 Goggles for eye protection.

14 Stippling brush for stippling small areas.

15 Assorted brushes for paint and varnish.

16 Variety of sandpapers.

17 Dust mask for lung protection.

18 Paper scraps for testing paint colors.

Preparing surfaces

BEFORE YOU BEGIN TO DECORATE YOUR HOUSE, IT IS VERY IMPORTANT TO CHECK THE ENTIRE SURFACE, LOOKING FOR GAPS WHERE PANELS MEET, NAIL HOLES, KNOTS, BLEMISHES IN THE GRAIN, OR ANY OTHER SCARS, DENTS, AND SO ON THAT MAY SHOW THROUGH THE DECORATION.

There is nothing worse than spending hours decorating, only to find afterward that some imperfection is spoiling the effect. Although the vast majority of kits and ready-made houses are well produced, there is always some detail that requires attention. A common problem with some kits is that the panels are cut slightly out of true, resulting in gaps that must be filled and rubbed down. Make sure when filling that you force the putty into the gaps, leaving the paste slightly above the surface so that you can sand it perfectly flat. Be sure to check the inside of the house as well as the outside; in particular, check the joint where the back panel meets the sides and where the roof is joined to the main walls.

PREPARATION

Any gaps, holes, and dents should be filled with good-quality wood putty in accordance with manufacturer's instructions. If you are painting on porous wood, you should first prime the surface using a commercial primer as instructed. The primer may "lift" the surface grain, so sand it afterward using fine-grit sandpaper. The particleboard used for most dollhouses has a closed surface and no grain, so priming may not be required. Try a small area on the back or underside to check for suction. Use good-quality materials; the results will need to last for years to come. Check every inch of the house and be sure that all preparation is completed before you begin to decorate.

YOU WILL NEED
Good-quality wood putty
Putty knife or spatula
Nail punch
Oil paint
Primer
Sandpaper
Brushes
Mineral spirits
Hammer

1 | Check all angles and corners for protruding nails. Any found should be punched in using a nail punch and small hammer. Use light strokes to avoid damage to the joints.

TIPS OF THE TRADE
If you don't have any scraps of wood, use the underside of the house, which won't be seen, to test any paint or stain colors before decoration.

2 | When all nails have been punched in, cover all nail holes with a little oil-based paint. This will seal the nail heads and prevent rust from showing through the finish.

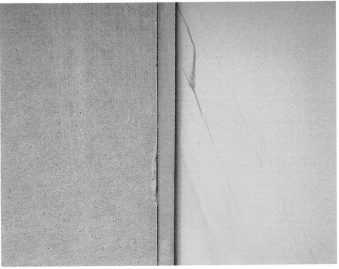

3 | Although uncommon, you may find that the panels of your house don't fit together as well as they might. Such gaps will spoil any decorative finish.

4 | Mix wood putty to a thick paste and let it stand for a few moments. Fill in any nail holes or gaps, using a plastic spatula or putty knife, forcing putty into the gap. If the putty shows through on the other side, wipe it off with a damp cloth.

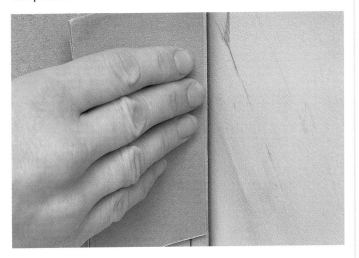

5 | When the putty is properly dry, sand it to a smooth, even finish, first with medium-grit sandpaper, then with fine grit. Wipe away any dust using a slightly damp cloth.

Fixtures and fittings

THE MINIATURE FIXTURES AND
FITTINGS IN A DOLLHOUSE OFTEN
PROVIDE THE AUTHENTIC TOUCHES
THAT BRING THE WHOLE EFFECT TO LIFE.

◄ Solid brass door hardware is widely available through dollhouse and model-making suppliers. This selection includes the following: Georgian door knocker, Victorian door plate set, internal brass door knob, and a pair of Victorian french door handles.

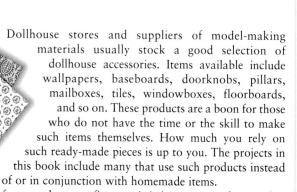

Dollhouse stores and suppliers of model-making materials usually stock a good selection of dollhouse accessories. Items available include wallpapers, baseboards, doorknobs, pillars, mailboxes, tiles, windowboxes, floorboards, and so on. These products are a boon for those who do not have the time or the skill to make such items themselves. How much you rely on such ready-made pieces is up to you. The projects in this book include many that use such products instead of or in conjunction with homemade items.

Before you buy any fixtures, it is important to know what you are looking for. As with other aspects of dollhouse decoration, research in the correct style of item for the period will always pay off in terms of the quality of the final effect. Making sure that the products you buy are in the correct scale is equally important.

If you are lucky enough to live close to a good supplier, you can view the accessories before you buy, which can be a great advantage. However, for those who do not have a local outlet, or if you want access to a greater choice of products than you can obtain at your nearby store, many companies operate a mail order service. Before ordering by mail, be sure to find out if you will incur any additional costs for postage and packing and what the company's returns policy is.

JOINING A CLUB Miniaturists clubs are another good source of dollhouse accessories. You can often find great ideas in their newsletters as well as details of new suppliers. Many clubs also hold regular meetings and workshops, which provide a highly enjoyable way of broadening your knowledge.

▲ These ornate brass fixtures have much fine detailing and are suitable for use on a grand house.

▲ This selection represents only a few examples of the vast selection of dollhouse light fixtures available. They are as follows: a simple hanging lamp, a Victorian-style ceiling lamp with chains, and a grand three-arm hurricane chandelier.

▼ Table lamps make a great contribution to a finished room, adding a warm glow. This selection includes a hurricane lamp, a brass lamp with a fluted shade, and a banker's desk lamp with traditional green shade.

▲ The following items are made by plaster casting: large ornate corbel, small plain corbel, a hampton ceiling medallion, and a grapeleaf ceiling rose.

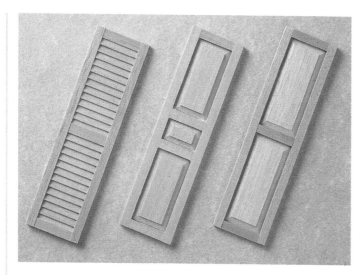

◄ Wooden shutters are more common in out-of-town houses, but are also sometimes used in cities. Do a little research to see if they would be practical and appropriate on your house. The examples shown here are a typical louvered design, three-panel "Americana" shutter, and a two-panel Jamestown shutter.

▲ Add a little detail to the front of your house with an apex trim. There are many styles available, and they come in various sizes. This trim with its elaborate detailing is designed to fit into all 45-degree apexes (the point at which both halves of the roof meet).

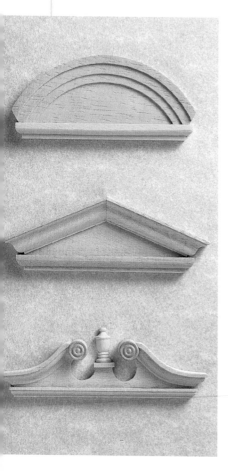

◄ Window pediments add a certain refinement to any dollhouse. They are available in many styles and are simply glued in place after painting. The pictured examples are a Federal circle, a Federal hooded design, and for the ultimate window dressing, a Deerfield pediment, with its delicately scrolled design and intricate detail.

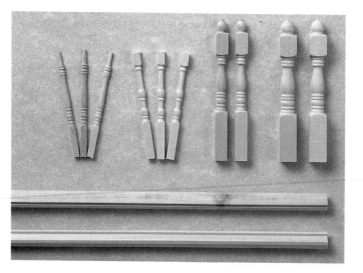

◄ A porch at the front of the house or a balcony under the windows provide distinction to a dollhouse exterior. All the component parts illustrated here are easily available: wooden spindles for porch or staircase, newel posts for the ends, and top and bottom rails to take spindles. Check that your spindles fit into the rails correctly before purchase.

▲ All but the most modern of houses need chimneys. Chimneys can be made quite simply from a block of wood cut to suit the pitch of the roof, or they can be bought ready-made. Shown here is an example of a ready-made stack topped with an ornamental hood.

◄▲ Fireplaces can be the focal point in any room. They can, however, be quite expensive, particularly if you need one in each room. Here we show three examples of unfinished fireplaces for you to decorate yourself, thereby cutting the cost dramatically.

▲ Chimneypots are available made from many materials. However, terra-cotta pots are the most authentic. They are not too expensive if you don't need many. The pots shown are actually flowerpots, which are half the price of chimneypots.

► For a country cottage or farmhouse, a picket fence with a gate provides an appropriate boundary. You can buy these already made or you can easily make your own. Use wooden stirring sticks with the round ends cut off. Glue them to a top and bottom rail to create your fence.

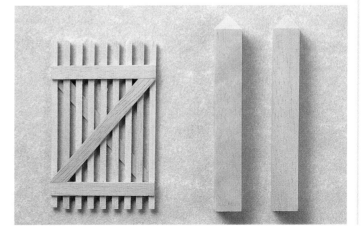

INTERIOR WALLS

Antiquing

ANTIQUING IS USED ON DOLLHOUSE
FURNISHINGS, FRAMES, AND FAÇADES,
SIMULATING THE PROCESS OF AGING
AND WEATHERING OF TIME. THIS
AGING EFFECT CAN ADD HISTORICAL
CHARACTER AND A LIVED-IN FEELING
TO BOTH OLD AND NEW DOLLHOUSES.

Antiquing makes new wood look old and is effective on various furnishings, dados, moldings, wooden panels, and wooden floorboards. The keys to success lie in a well-prepared surface, and a subtle use of color.

When applying the color stain, make sure the wood is fairly porous. Most wooden moldings are available from dollhouse stores, modelmaker's suppliers, and miniature specialists. They are usually bought untreated; however, if you are antiquing premade furniture or working from kits, you will need to clean it with denatured alcohol and sand it with fine steel wool or fine sandpaper. Some furniture and dollhouse kits are made of plastic, and certain wood stains will work well on these surfaces, so even a modern material can be made to look old.

Earth colors, such as burnt umber, raw umber, raw sienna, and burnt sienna, are normally used for antiquing. Acrylic paints are recommended because they dry quickly. You can mix varnish with an acrylic medium with a flat or gloss finish, depending on the required look. If you prefer a high gloss varnish with a yellowing brownish hue, you can use shellac varnish as a final varnish. If the shellac is too thick, thin it with denatured alcohol. To give you extra drying time when you are working on a larger scale, such as a façade, use an oil glaze. To extend your color range, mix warmer pigment into the final glaze. Earth colors can sometimes look rather dull unless you use the warmer range like burnt sienna or raw sienna, once it is mixed with a transparent glaze.

☞

Quoining, page 90

YOU WILL NEED
For use with acrylic only
Sandpaper
Soft cloth
Earth color acrylic paints
Acrylic matt medium
Paintbrushes
1in and ½in flat varnish
  brush
File
Shellac or matt acrylic
  varnish

ANTIQUING
Antiquing is a valuable technique that can be used to make sure that the effect of a period-style dollhouse is not undermined by modern-looking furniture. Here, a new drop-leaf table is treated to give it the authentic appearance of old oak.

1 | Sand the furniture with fine sandpaper, working along the grain of the wood until the existing varnish is removed. If the furniture is unvarnished, just rub lightly with sandpaper to create a "tooth" on the wood.

2 | Mix raw umber and burnt sienna acrylic paint with acrylic matt medium to obtain a semitransparent consistency. Apply to the furniture with a 1in flat brush.

3 | Wrap a piece of lint-free cloth around your index finger. Working in a circular motion, rub the paint into the wood until the furniture is completely covered.

5 | Rub away any excess paint with a clean, lint-free cloth. Certain areas will be lighter in tone due to the varying absorbency of the wood. The darkest areas will be in the grooves and recesses.

7 | Use a ½in brush to add some darker tones of raw umber. This will accentuate the indentations, adding to the authentic antique finish.

4 | Use a small brush to move the paint into the corners. Paint into the carved areas on the legs and underneath the table top.

6 | When the paint is dry, gently use a file to create a few grooves and indentations in the wood to give the appearance of decades of wear and tear.

8 | Finally, varnish the surface. Use shellac for a high-gloss, warm finish or matt acrylic varnish if a shine is not desired.

9 | The finished item has the rich patina associated with old well-loved furniture.

Antiquing techniques are invaluable for creating dollhouses with a period feel. The examples shown here include interior and exterior features that have been treated to give an aged appearance.

1 This Victorian-style ceiling rose would provide a stylish finishing touch to any 19th-century interior. These can be bought from good dollhouse suppliers and painted as appropriate. In this example, brown paint has been brushed into the molding to avoid the impression of newness that would have been conveyed by unmodified white paint.

2 Over time most exterior finishes will show the effects of weathering, and this can be imitated in a dollhouse by antiquing the brick or stonework. These quoin stones have been painted to give the impression of moss and lichen on old stone.

3 Choosing the right color of wood for the furniture and woodwork of the room you are creating is a vital element in achieving a historical feel. Here, a variegated effect using raw umber and raw sienna glazes results in a wood color that would be suitable for a Tudor or Jacobean interior.

4 Like interior decorations, garden ornaments can be treated to antiquing effects. This terracotta urn has been brushed with green paint and chalk to convey the effect of weathering. It would look appropriate on a front porch or in the dollhouse garden.

Blocking designs

BLOCKING DESIGN IS A WAY OF ACHIEVING A

REPEAT PATTERN THROUGH THE USE OF BLOCK

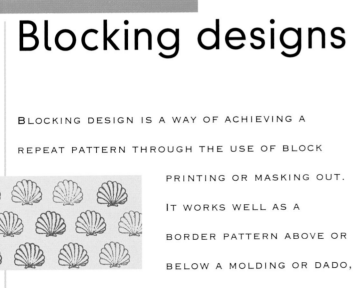

PRINTING OR MASKING OUT.

IT WORKS WELL AS A

BORDER PATTERN ABOVE OR

BELOW A MOLDING OR DADO,

AND WHEN DECORATING WOODEN FURNITURE.

MASK BLOCKING CREATES LINEAR PATTERNS AND

IS A QUICK WAY OF ACHIEVING HARD-EDGED

PATTERNS OR SHAPES.

Printing from wooden blocks is one of the earliest methods of relief printing, going as far back as the 8th century. The printing blocks were normally hand-carved, but carving your own designs can be time-consuming and daunting if you are a beginner. Instead purchase some pre-carved printing blocks or rubber printing stamps. It is possible to buy small wooden blocks which are sealed with a thin sheet of etched copper to form a relief image. There are a whole range of designs to choose from, and they are just the right scale for dollhouses; however, be prepared to hunt around at craft fairs, antique stores, or yard sales to find them.

INKING THE BLOCKS To ink the blocks, you need tubes of water-based printing inks or thick-bodied acrylics. If you are printing on fabric, you can buy small jars of fabric paints from most art-supply stores. Apply paint with a paintbrush rather than dipping the block in the paint, as this can be messy. Wipe off any excess ink or paint from the block, especially around the edges, then do a few sample prints before committing yourself to the final surface. If you are block printing on wooden furniture or paneling, apply a coat of varnish when the prints are dry.

MASKING This is a form of blocking or stopping out, using strips of masking tape. You can buy masking tape in a variety of widths from ¼in to 2in. The areas covered by the tape are protected from paint applied to the unmasked areas. This technique allows you to create clean, straight lines and edges, and may be helpful when painting a *trompe l'oeil* scene (see p.40).

Stripes on walls can make interesting wallpaper effects – for example, mimicking Regency stripes or modern optical patterns. Always use contrasting colors for best results.

When using this technique, always make sure that the paint has a thick finish and does not seep through the masking tape. If this happens, the paint consistency is too runny. When the paint is almost dry, peel off the tape. It will peel off a wooden surface easily. On paper there is a risk that removing the tape will tear the surface, so always use low-tack tape and peel it off slowly.

☞
Preparing the surface,
page 16
Stenciling, page 51

YOU WILL NEED
Rubber stamp blocking
Marker pen
Rubber block
Carving tool
Ink or paint
Ink pad
Paintbrush
Paper
Ruler and pencil
Clean cloth

BLOCKING ONTO PAPER WITH RUBBER STAMPS
Rubber stamps are easier to carve than wooden blocks. A rubber stamp kit is perfect for making your own miniature block prints. You can print onto most surfaces, but the technique works best on a slightly absorbent surface such as paper, primed wood, or fabric. Before you draw your design on the rubber, make a few sketches on paper. Keep your design bold and simple.

1 Draw your design onto the rubber stamp with a permanent marker pen. Try to keep the image to an appropriate scale and keep your design simple. Use tracing paper if you find it difficult to draw directly onto the rubber.

2 | Carefully carve into the rubber stamp, working away from you. Cut away the negative space surrounding the image.

4 | Apply ink to the pad. Use a paintbrush to avoid over-loading the pad and make sure the ink is not too runny.

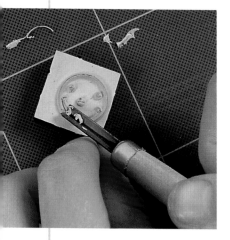

3 | Carve into the stamp to a depth of about ⅛in. Make a test print to see if you need to cut deeper.

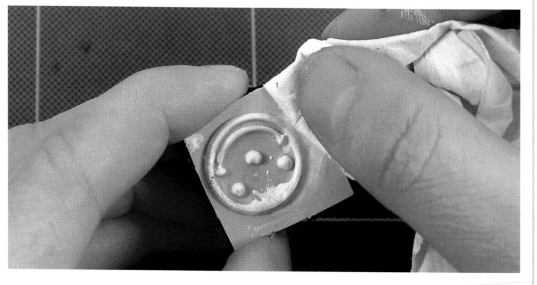

5 | Wipe away any excess paint from the rubber stamp with a dry cloth.

6 | Press the rubber stamp onto the inked pad. Make sure the whole of the image is covered with ink.

7 | Use a ruler and pencil to measure and lightly mark the intended position of each print on the paper.

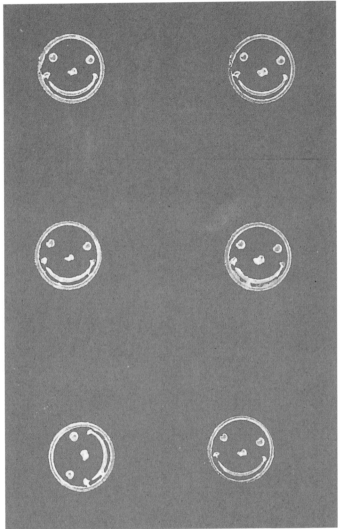

9 | The finished paper would add a cheerful touch to a child's bedroom, either as wallpaper or applied to a piece of furniture.

8 | Print the image onto the paper. Make sure the rubber stamp is clean around the edges after each re-inking. to achieve a precise series of prints.

BLOCKING ONTO FURNITURE WITH A RUBBER STAMP

The surface of the furniture to be printed should be unvarnished and primed with either white gesso or acrylic paint. Sand with fine sandpaper between coats. After printing your design, you can seal with an acrylic varnish or shellac to achieve a warm gloss.

YOU WILL NEED
Blocking onto furniture
Paintbrush
Acrylic paint
Sandpaper
Stamp
Ink or paint
Pencil

1 | Paint the surface with the desired background color. When the paint is dry, lightly sand to a smooth surface.

2 | Use a ready-made stamp or cut your own. Apply paint to the stamp as described on page 28. Make sure the edges of the stamp are clean.

3 | Mark the intended position of the print in pencil on the furniture. Print your design directly onto the painted surface.

4 | This simple wooden table with pink frogs on a lime green background would be suitable for a child's nursery.

MASKING

This technique is a quick and precise way of applying a hard-edged linear pattern directly on the walls of your dollhouse. Always make sure that your base color is thoroughly dry before applying the tape. In this project contrasting tones within a similar color range have been used. If you want to achieve a subtle design, work with a limited palette of subtle gradations of color. This design works well above or below a dado. Applied to an entire room, the effect could be too busy. It works best when contrasted with a flat color.

YOU WILL NEED
Hard-edged patterns
Low-tack masking tape
Nylon paintbrushes
Utility knife
Straightedge
Pencil
Paper
Clean cloth
Acrylic paints or water-based printing inks
Small jars for mixing paint

1 | Draw the dado level with a ruler and a pencil and then apply a strip of masking tape above the marked line. Apply strips of tape from the floor to the dado level. Use a sharp utility knife to trim to length. Press the tape on firmly with your fingertips. This is very important because the tape needs to be stuck to the wall securely to prevent the paint from bleeding underneath.

2 | Remove alternate strips of tape with care to avoid peeling off the paint underneath.

4 | When the paint is dry, add another strip of masking tape over each painted area, leaving a ⅛in vertical strip along one edge exposed.

5 | Apply darker paint over these thin stripes using a ⅜in flat brush. Work quickly.

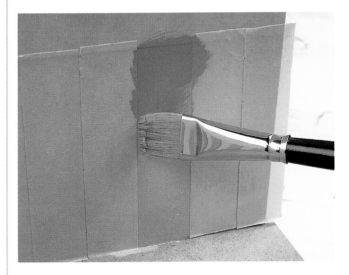

3 | Using a flat 1in brush, paint the contrasting color over the exposed areas. Make sure the masking tape is securely pressed to the wall. The paint should be a thick, creamy consistency, applied using strokes in one direction only.

6 | When all the thin stripes have been painted and are dry, peel off the tape. You may notice some of the lines are not perfectly hard-edged because the paint may have seeped through the tape slightly.

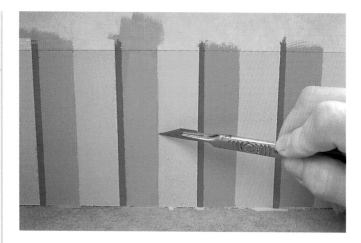

9 | Remove all the remaining masking tape. To define the top edge of the pattern, you can add either a paper border or a dado. The border pattern shown is taken from a découpage miniatures book. Cut out the thin strips with a utility knife and a ruler. Stick the border to the wall with wallpaper paste, removing all air bubbles. When dry, trim off any excess with the knife.

7 | Remove the excess paint to clean up the edges by scraping the surface lightly with a sharp utility knife.

8 | Repaint the scraped-off areas with a ⅜in brush. Keep a steady hand and work slowly and accurately. Make sure the color is a good match; otherwise, the brush marks will be noticeable.

10 | The bedroom setting mixes the old with the new, combining Victorian mahogany furniture with a contemporary wall design. Stenciling instructions are given on page 50.

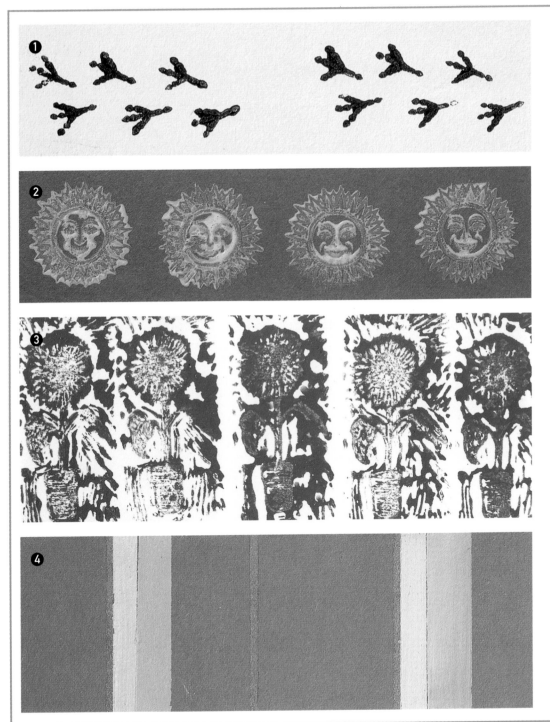

Blocking designs provide the opportunity for fun designs on walls and furniture. However, the various blocking techniques can also be adapted for use as formal borders around cornices and along dado rails.

❶ A rubber stamp pattern of bird's feet would make an ideal decorative border in a child's room. Here a subdued combination of black on peach has been used, but a livelier effect could be achieved with a combination of bright primary colors.

❷ A sun motif printed in gold on a rich blue background creates a wonderfully opulent effect. The irregularities that are an integral part of the method add to the individuality of the effect.

❸ Printed with red oxide paint, this sunflower design rubber stamp produces a highly rustic effect. It could be used successfully in conjunction with a stone-flagged floor in a farmhouse kitchen.

❹ Striped patterns on walls can be easily produced using a masking technique. By using stripes of different widths in carefully chosen colors, you can create original effects to suit any room in your dollhouse.

Découpage

YOU WILL NEED
For a wall
Images reduced to size
Utility knife
White craft glue
1in brush
Varnish

DÉCOUPAGE IS A DECORATIVE TECHNIQUE USED FOR COVERING FURNITURE, ORNAMENTS, AND OBJECTS TO GIVE THE EFFECT OF HANDPAINTING. IT IS A GREAT TECHNIQUE TO USE IN A DOLLHOUSE BECAUSE IT IS EASY TO DO AND THE RESULTS ARE VERY SATISFYING.

Découpage derives from the French term "decouper" meaning to cut up or cut out paper, and it is the art of cutting out paper shapes with scissors and pasting them down to make a collage design. Découpage was very popular in Victorian England, so historically it works well in Victorian-style houses. When using this technique, always be aware of the scale; the cutout images must be the right size. Start collecting wrapping papers and Victorian prints for images that are fairly close to dollhouse scale.

Once you have cut out the pieces, arrange them on the object or furnishing, making sure that the composition fits. The adjoining edges of the paper cutouts should fit together a bit like a jigsaw puzzle fitting edge to edge. Then glue the cutouts in place; aerosol glue is a good adhesive to use on miniatures because it has a clean finish and does not leave any blobs of oozing glue to clean up. White craft glue is an acceptable alternative. The final stage involves sealing the découpage with varnish. If you want an antique finish, you can add some earth color paints, such as burnt umber or burnt sienna, to the varnish. This creates a lacquering effect which produces a high gloss finish. Shellac is a good medium to use with découpage because it is quick drying and results in a transparent brown sheen.

☞
Preparing the surface,
page 16
Handmade wallpapers,
page 62
Print room technique,
page 48
Varnishing, page 60

DÉCOUPAGE DECORATION ON A WALL

Découpage decoration is more effective around a door frame or a window than covering an entire wall. The decorative collage adds color and pattern that can transform a plain wall. The découpage pieces should always be applied to a pre-painted wall. Make sure that your choice of wall color complements your découpage pieces to create a harmonious color scheme.

1 | Fresh floral images have been chosen for this découpage design. These have been reduced on a color photocopier. Cut out the pieces with a utility knife.

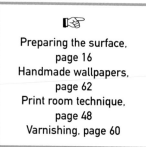

5 | Once the découpage is complete, hang the door in place.

2 | Arrange the pieces on the wall to create a pleasing decorative effect.

3 | When you are happy with the arrangement, glue the pieces in position with white craft glue.

4 | When the glue is dry, seal the collage with glue or varnish. This will also prevent the colors from fading over time.

6 | Finished example. In the completed room, the cedar-red furniture contrasts boldly with the black and white diamond-pattern floor. The red door echoes the red of the flowers, and the yellow wall contributes to a fresh summer look.

DECOUPAGING FURNITURE

The traditional art of découpage can enliven a dull piece of furniture or be used to disguise damaged areas. The effects are as varied as the images available. Although working with tiny pieces of paper can be time-consuming and a little tedious, the reward is a unique item that adds a touch of individuality to your dollhouse.

YOU WILL NEED
For furniture
Spray adhesive
Scissors
Utility knife
Cutting mat
White craft glue
Round hog's-hair brush for gluing
Magazines, Victorian prints or wrapping papers
Acrylic gloss medium
Shellac or synthetic lacquer
Varnish brush

1 │ The first consideration is the style of images to be used. Choose a theme that is in keeping with the style and period of the furniture. Victorian prints are a popular choice for a historical look. However, contemporary designs should be used on modern furniture. Reduce the images on a color photocopier to obtain the size you require.

3 │ Place the surface of the furniture to be decorated face down on a thin piece of cardboard. Draw around the shape and cut out the shape with a utility knife to make the template. Arrange the cutout images on the template before finally gluing them to the furniture.

4 │ Apply white craft glue or an aerosol glue to the surface of the furniture to be decorated. Following the design of your template, transfer the cutout images to the glued surface. Smooth them with your fingertips to make sure that the pieces stick firmly. Let them dry.

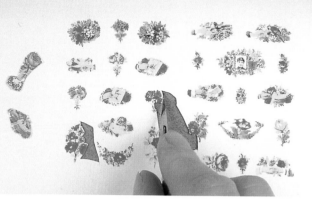

2 │ Use a utility knife to cut out the images. This can be quite awkward on such a small scale. A sharp knife helps, so make sure your blades are changed regularly.

5 │ Paint a coat of acrylic gloss medium over the decorated surface. The medium works as a sealant and varnish, protecting the images and preventing the colors from fading.

6 | When the acrylic medium is dry, apply a thin coat of shellac. This transparent sepia varnish helps to achieve the authentic look of the Victorian period. Shellac is quick drying and hard wearing. Clean your varnish brush immediately after use in denatured alcohol and then use olive oil soap to keep the bristles soft.

Floral designs are a very popular découpage theme. They have a romantic feel and look great with pastel paintwork. There is a large selection of floral wrapping paper designs to choose from. You will need to photocopy your images to a 1–12 scale so select several sheets in a bold, good quality design.

This floral découpage with a butterfly will enliven a piece of furniture. The choice of design will also work well as a creative border around a doorway or a window.

When reduced to 1–12 scale, birds and botanical subjects could work well in a dollhouse bathroom, on a door or around a window frame or mirror. They bring a touch of nature to a domestic environment.

Découpaged roses can give a room or an object a touch of romance and can be used to decorate a Victorian screen, an ornate ceramic vase, or a border around a room or fireplace.

7 | The finished table has a subtle sheen imparted by the shellac.

Handpainted walls

HANDPAINTED WALLS ARE THE FIRST STEP TOWARD DECORATING YOUR DOLLHOUSE. THE FIRST COAT OF PAINT WORKS AS A PRIMER, SEALING THE WOOD, WHILE THE SECOND WORKS AS A BASE COAT FOR MORE INTRICATE DECORATING WORK.

Before you start any handpainting, make sure that the walls are free of lumps, holes, and dust (see page 16). Always remove all windows and doors so that the house is an empty shell; you will find it much easier to paint without having to negotiate tricky corners and angles. Refer to your room plan as you are painting; this will save you from doing any unnecessary painting which may later be covered with wallpaper or paneling.

ORDER OF WORK The inside of a dollhouse is usually painted with white latex paint as the first priming coat. Before you start, cover all the electrical outlets with masking tape to avoid clogging the holes with paint. Start with the ceiling. The base coat will vary according to the color scheme of each room; this coat is painted with vinyl silk latex paint because it is easier to clean, it dries quickly, and the sheen reflects more light than flat latex.

Working on the outside of the dollhouse, the first exterior coat is also done in flat latex, usually an appropriate undercoat color, which is then covered with textured paint or finish.

☞
Preparing the surface,
page 16
Textured external paint
finishes, page 92
Wallpapering, page 66

TROMPE L'OEIL *Trompe l'oeil* is a French term meaning to deceive or fool the eye. This technique allows you to create illusory spaces and scenes—a dramatic alternative to wallpaper or paint.

Mural painting relies heavily on the effect of *tromp l'oeil*, and through the use of mural decoration on a miniature scale, you can transform a dining room into a splendid exotic garden or a nursery into a fairytale landscape. *Tromp l'oeil* brings realism and grandeur to a dollhouse. This effect can be handpainted or you can purchase *trompe l'oeil* prints from dollhouse suppliers. Obviously handpainting is more fun, and it allows you to create your own designs. The scenes depicted range from Versailles gardens, views through windows, and illusions of real paintings in their frames, to sculptures and classical columns. Although the themes are wide-ranging, they do tend to have an historical or romantic feel.

WHERE TO USE TROMP L'OEIL You need not paint an entire room; the *trompe l'oeil* effect will work equally well in alcoves, over doors, or to suggest false ceilings and floors. If you find handpainting difficult, use printed papers. Miniature painting involves a lot of patience and skill, and you will need to have a basic grasp of perspective. Visual reference is essential for this technique; collect images from magazines and catalogs. Home decorating magazines and books on *trompe l'oeil* and perspective will stimulate ideas. You may have a favorite theme or landscape that can be filtered into your decorative scheme. The quality of finish will depend on your painting skills, so bear this in mind before you start.

Try to keep the design simple but effective, achieving a concept of space through contrasting lights and darks and linear perspective. Work with the features already in the room, such as doors and windows. It is these areas where real space can interact with the illusory work. A door may be turned into a grand entrance, for example, or you could paint a false door or window into a room, opening onto an imagined space.

HANDPAINTING
Painted walls are an easy way of adding color to the rooms of your dollhouse. You can paint the ceiling and walls the same color, or you may decide to use two or more colors, depending on the desired effect. Painted walls also provide the starting point for several more elaborate forms of decoration.

YOU WILL NEED
Handpainting tools
½in, 1in, and 2in paintbrushes
Silk finish latex paint
Vinyl flat latex paint

4 ┃ When all the painting is finished, peel off the masking tape to uncover the electric outlets. Sand any noticeable lumps with fine sandpaper. The walls are now ready for embellishment with other decorative finishes.

1 ┃ Cover all electric outlets with masking tape to prevent paint from clogging the holes. If you are painting adjacent walls a different color, it is a good idea to put masking tape along the edge where the walls meet. Use low-tack masking tape to reserve any areas you are leaving unpainted. This helps to create clean edges and prevents lumps and drips from forming. If you are wallpapering the walls but want the ceiling to be painted, do not worry about paint extending onto the adjacent wall; simply rub it with sandpaper and then paper over it.

2 ┃ Mix the paint thoroughly before you start and remove any lumps. A flat 2in brush is suitable, or you could use a flat painting sponge, as shown here. This creates a very smooth finish and has the advantage of leaving no loose hairs. However, you may need to use a 1in flat brush to paint in the corners. Do not overload your brush or painting sponge, as this can cause drips. Paint the ceilings first. Apply the paint with even strokes in one direction only, to avoid visible brush marks.

The color you choose to paint walls and ceilings can dictate the mood and feel of each room. White is neutral, allowing you to use lively colors in other features of the room, while pastel shades can provide a warm, cool, or fresh feel, depending on the color chosen.

❶ White is the perfect base color for all interior walls. A white base coat seals the walls and ceilings, before the addition of wallpapers and contrasting color schemes. Ceilings are usually best left white, which maintains a neutrality within the room and will not clash with lively walls and complex architectural features. White is also perfect for windows, doors, baseboards, and cornices.

❷ Pastel pink is a romantic warm color. It is perfect for a child's bedroom, especially when used in combination with white, which gives a feeling of purity. Rose pink is also suitable for an adult's bedroom and complements pastel blue and rose garland wallpaper. As a base color, pink can be enlivened with stencils, blocking designs, and découpage.

❸ A blue palette is cool, calm, and space-creating. Rich blues stir the imagination and look great with golds, yellows, and orange-reds. Bathrooms, hallways, and ceilings are the perfect location for the use of blue in your dollhouse.

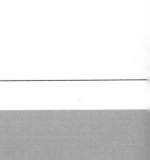

3 ┃ Walls usually need two coats of paint. The first coat of flat latex paint works as an undercoat, sealing the walls. The second coat is painted in a silk finish latex paint, which gives a slight sheen and is easy to clean. You may need to sand between each coat.

A TROMP L'OEIL INTERIOR

Drawing and painting skills are helpful for successful *trompe l'oeil* effects. Use sketches to develop your ideas, giving thought to both content and color. You can draw inspiration from paintings, photographs, or your own observations.

YOU WILL NEED
For tromp l'oeil painting
Stretched paper
Pencil
Ruler
Visual reference
Acrylic paints
Paintbrushes

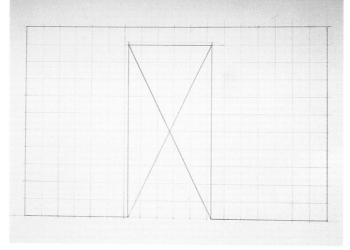

3 | Start to draw your *trompe l'oeil* scene in pencil. The more detail you include at this stage, the easier it will be to add color later. Refer to your visual reference as you work.

4 | You may get new ideas as you develop your drawing. Always consider how such additions will enhance the illusion. For example, in this drawing, the addition of drapery around the door accentuates the illusion of depth through its contrasting scale with the detail on the distant horizon.

2 | When you have drawn the outlines of the wall and any doors and windows, lightly draw a grid of 1in squares in pencil over the wall area. This will help you to copy your reference accurately.

1 | Once you have developed your idea, make an accurate full-size drawing of the wall or part of the room on stretched paper (see Stretching, p.44). Make sure the paper is large enough to accommodate the dimensions of the wall, window, or other area you are drawing. Mark any door or window openings in the wall on your drawing. Accurate measuring is essential.

5 | When the drawing is complete, you can start to add color. Using acrylics, start by adding your base color. This will act as your middle tone, which you can darken or lighten as necessary to create the illusion of depth. Use a ½in flat brush, and apply a thin first layer, building up the opacity as you develop the painting.

6 | Try to keep the effect simple, achieving a sense of depth through contrasting light and darks and the use of linear perspective. These are the basic elements of a convincing illusion. Remember that cool colors, such as blues, recede and warm colors, such as reds and oranges, come forward.

7 | When the painting is finished and thoroughly dry, paste the paper to the wall as if it were wallpaper (see p.66). Cut out the door when the glue is dry. If the door is too big for the space allowed in your design, you can trim further back. However, if the space left for the door is too small, you may be able to conceal any gaps with a wide door frame. The *tromp l'oeil* illusion is created by tricking the eye, thus creating a landscape beyond the door. The color scheme of the room and the door is reflected in the painting, adding to the illusion of the image.

Faux marbling

FAUX MARBLING IS USED IN
DOLLHOUSES TO DECORATE
ARCHITECTURAL FEATURES,
FIREPLACES, MARBLE-TOPPED
FURNITURE, INTERIOR PANELING,
WALLS, AND FLOORING. THIS TECHNIQUE GIVES A
GRANDIOSE FINISH, ENLIVENING EVEN THE MOST
ORDINARY DOLLHOUSE INTERIOR WITH THE SUBTLE
PATTERNING OF A MARBLE SURFACE.

The technique of faux marbling dates back to the ancient Egyptians and has subsequently been passed through many generations. Even in France and Italy, where marble is readily available, the copying of the true material has been popular. This is because of the high cost of marble and the impracticality of working with such an expensive and bulky medium.

Faux marbling was very popular in French baroque-style interiors and Regency palaces. Its grand style has been a recurrent theme among miniaturists who imitate as closely as possible authentic marble surfaces. Real marble would be very impractical to work with on the scale of dollhouses, so the painted technique is an effective solution. When planning an interior, it is useful to look at different authentic marbles, and study their pattern and veining, while keeping in mind the color combinations you wish to incorporate into your interior. Then you could simply copy a marble that appeals to you, or experiment with your own colors. Practice the technique before committing your final design to paper.

☞
Preparing the surface,
page 16
Varnishing, page 60

APPLICATIONS Your choice of color and depth will create different atmospheres. A pale marble may suit a kitchen, whereas a more exotic dark marble may give character to a bathroom or dining room. Marbling can be applied to flat surfaces, for example wallpaper, work surfaces, or meat counters, as well as three-dimensional areas such as paneling, columns, and furniture. When working on a three-dimensional surface, practice your finish on a piece of dowel or wood before decorating the final surface.

USING PREPRINTED MARBLE WALLPAPERS

You can buy marble papers from many decorator's suppliers as well as specialist decorative paper suppliers. Many different designs and colors are available. Some papers are self-adhesive; others need to be pasted.

YOU WILL NEED

For preprinted papers
Particleboard panels
White craft glue
Utility knife
Marble wallpaper or self-adhesive marble paper
Wallpaper paste
2in flat brush
Metal rule

1 | First measure the wall of your room. Cut the paper to the required size with a utility knife and metal rule, adding an extra ⅛in all around, as it is always better to have too much paper than too little. You can trim off the excess later when the paper is dry.

2 | Apply wallpaper paste to the back of the paper with a flat brush.

3 | Then apply paste to the wall. Make sure the wall is evenly pasted all over; otherwise, air bubbles may appear.

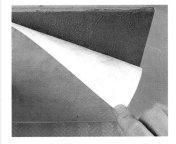

4 | Place the paper on the wall. Smooth it with your hands to remove any air bubbles.

5 | The paper should meet at the corners, concealing any seams. Fold over any excess and trim with a sharp knife when the paper is dry.

6 | Make marble panels in a different color using self-adhesive marble paper. Cut the panels from particleboard.

7 | Cut the self-adhesive marble paper to fit the panels. Peel off the adhesive backing.

8 | Stick the marble paper to the panel. Glue the panel to the wall with white craft glue. Secure the panel to the wall with a small clamp or masking tape while the glue is drying .

9 | Columns and baseboards can be added to enhance the classical effect.

STRETCHING PAPER

Stretching the paper prevents it from wrinkling when wet paint is applied. The quality of finish and saturation of color is further improved if you prime the stretched paper with gesso, because this prevents the paint from sinking into the paper.

YOU WILL NEED
For stretching paper
Smooth, flat drawing board
Gummed tape
Sponge
Warm water
Typing paper
Scissors

2 Place the lengths of gummed tape along the edges of the paper so that half the width overlaps onto the board. Smooth the tape and the paper to release the air bubbles and any creases.

MARBLING STRETCHED PAPER USING OIL PAINT

Paper painted to resemble marble can be applied to a wide variety of surfaces such as walls, floors, and raised panels. It can also be applied to furniture. The marble shown has a delicately figured pattern. Stretch your paper before painting the marble effect.

YOU WILL NEED
For paper
Gesso primer
Smooth flat board
½in flat brush
Oil paints, tubes
White undercoat paint
Transparent oil glaze
Watercolor brushes ranging
  from 0–6
Natural sponge
Hog's-hair brush
Mineral spirits
Oil-based varnish
Pure turpentine
Soft brush
Paper towels

1 Cut typing paper to the desired size. Wet the paper evenly so that it is moist but not dripping wet. Place it on the board. Cut four lengths of gummed tape longer than the sides of the paper. Dip these in a bowl of warm water.

3 Wipe off any excess water with a damp sponge. Then leave to dry. As the paper dries, it should stretch to a smooth unwrinkled finish.

1 Seal the stretched paper with a gesso acrylic primer. Then apply a white oil-based undercoat on top of the acrylic gesso. Tint the white paint with a touch of raw sienna oil paint. Never use oil directly on unprimed paper because the oil will sink into the paper and eventually rot it. Small cans of white oil paint can be purchased from most hardware stores.

2 While the ground is still wet, mix three oil glazes using Indian red, cadmium yellow, and light cobalt blue artist's oil paint. Thin the paint slightly with turpentine and an oil-based medium. Brush the three glazes in irregular patches onto the wet primed paper.

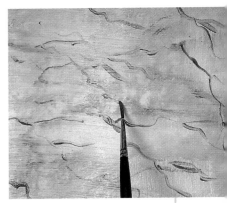

7 Blend the white areas with a broad brush before adding the finer detailed veins and highlights.

8 Use a fine watercolor brush to add more fine splintering veins, branching out from larger veins.

3 Blend the patches of color with a natural sponge, working the colors into the wet ground. This wet-in-wet blending technique creates subtle gradations of color.

5 Soften the veins with a broad, soft brush. If the brush becomes clogged with paint, wipe it with paper towels dampened with mineral spirits.

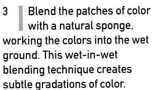

4 Mix ultramarine and black for the veining. Paint the detail with good-quality, fine watercolor brushes in a variety of sizes depending on the thickness of line required.

6 Soften the effect by adding patches of the white undercoat with a watercolor brush.

9 Add further highlights in white undercoat with a fine brush and blend with a sponge. Allow the completed design to dry and apply a thin oil-based varnish (see p.60). It is important to keep the varnish thin. Add some damar varnish to give a glossy finish. When it is dry, cut from the board with a utility knife and steel ruler.

MARBLING A COLUMN

In this project, marbling is applied to a piece of doweling to create a marble column. Lengths of doweling can be purchased from hardware stores. Alternatively, you can buy a broom handle and cut it to the appropriate size. When working on a small scale, it is best to avoid using oil paint unless you are confident with the medium. You may find the slow drying time difficult to control and end up with muddy colors. Acrylics are quick drying and can be diluted with water or with acrylic mediums and gels to create glazes. Acrylics and oils should not be mixed; however, oil can be applied on top of dry acrylic paint, but never the other way around. The key to successful marbling is blending, so work quickly. If you find this difficult, use a slow set medium.

YOU WILL NEED

For a column
Slow-set acrylic satin
    medium
Acrylic paints
Acrylic varnish
Natural sponge
1in flat brush
Watercolor brushes ranging
    from 0–6
Wooden dowel
    approximately 2in
    in diameter
Fine wet and dry sandpaper
Soft watercolor brush
Dry lint-free cloth
White gesso primer
½in brush

1 | Paint the column with a coat of white gesso primer. This prevents the next coat from sinking in. Leave it to dry, then sand with a piece of fine sandpaper. Mix white gesso with a little raw sienna acrylic paint to create a warm off-white color. Apply with a ½in brush, covering the white undercoat.

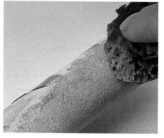

2 | While the second coat of gesso is still wet, mix three glazes using raw sienna, burnt sienna, and vermilion acrylic paints. Thin the paint slightly with slow-set acrylic medium. Use a fine brush to apply the glazes in irregular patches onto the wet dowel, turning the dowel as you apply to cover the entire surface area. Use a soft natural sponge to blend the colors into the wet ground.

3 | Mix ultramarine and black acrylics for the veining detail. Apply fine lines using good-quality watercolor brushes. Work quickly, drawing in branching veins. Bear in mind the scale and keep turning the dowel as you work.

4 | Soften the veins with the ½in flat brush, and blend with a soft brush and a little transparent acrylic slow-set medium. The veins will merge into the wet ground, creating a variety of subtle markings.

5 | Add patches of white paint between the drawn veins and then soften these white areas with a soft sable brush, working back and forth. Clean the brush with a dry cloth to prevent the paint from clogging the brush. The dark veins and the white patches should merge into each other to create a realistic marble effect.

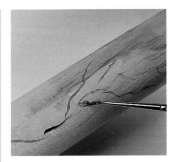

6 | Add a few fine veins to give a more detailed finish. Working to scale, apply these with a fine watercolor brush. Draw in a network of thin branching veins.

8 | Apply a thin oil-based varnish (see p.60) with a soft ½in brush. You may want to add a tiny touch of yellow ocher or warm Indian red to the varnish to give a warm color. It is important to keep the varnish to a thin consistency; you may need to dilute it with gloss acrylic medium. When the varnish is thoroughly dry, rub down very lightly with wet and dry sandpaper.

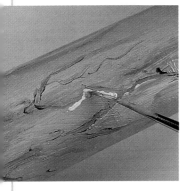

7 | Highlight the fine veins with a touch of white, then soften with a natural sponge. The marble shown is warm in color and has a delicately figured pattern that resembles pale marble. Leave the completed column to dry.

9 | This pair of faux marble columns function as an architectural support, adding a sense of opulence to the Grand style pedimented entrance.

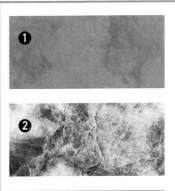

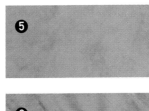

Marble is a wonderfully varied stone that has been used since ancient times. For dollhouses very convincing marble effects can be achieved with paint or by the use of printed marble papers. Real marble occurs in a wide range of colors, so you can choose color combinations to suit most situations.

❶ This blue and white marble was achieved with titanium white, cobalt blue, and ultramarine light added to a slow-set matt medium. This would suit a luxury bathroom.

❷ Created by using raw sienna, burnt umber, and vermillion with a white base, this is appropriate for columns, fireplaces, and furniture.

❸ This subtle gray marble would be ideal for a luxury flooring in a grand entrance hall of any building. The neutral colors would work well with bold colors and ornate furnishings. It uses Payne's gray and touches of Hooker's green in an oil or acrylic base.

❹ Dark gray marble could provide flooring as well as a functional surface in the kitchen or bathroom. This was achieved with white, black, and Payne's gray paint mixed with a transparent glaze.

❺ This bold contrasting marble could be used for baseboards, pillars, or table tops. It could also be contrasted with a paler marble in, say, an ornate fireplace. It utilizes white, Payne's gray, vermillion, black, and violet paint, mixed with acrylic or oil glaze.

❻ This green and white marble pattern is printed on self-adhesive sheets. Such papers generally have a glossy finish. They can be used on floors, walls, and table tops.

Print room technique

THE PRINT ROOM TECHNIQUE USES CUTOUT PAPER IMAGES TO CREATE A FUN AND CREATIVE ALTERNATIVE TO DECORATING WITH CONVENTIONAL MINIATURE WALLPAPERS.

The print room technique involves pasting paper scenes or portraits surrounded by paper frames onto a wall that is already decorated. This style of decoration first became popular in England in about 1754. At the time, it was an alternative to wallpaper, which was expensive because of heavy import taxes. The prints were usually taken from Old Master paintings, reproduced as woodcut prints and handpainted. Then they were pasted onto prepapered or painted walls.

This style of decoration will only work in certain rooms—such as a dining room, library, or study—as it can look quite elaborate. However, as you have free rein in choosing the pictures, the decoration will be personal—it will be your own miniature gallery. The spacing between each image needs to be carefully considered; always leave a gap of about ½–1in.

MAKING FRAMES If adding paper frames, try recycling images from interiors magazines or old catalogs. Frames can also be made out of decorative moldings or thin strips of wood; however, if you find this a little expensive, you can mount the paper images on cardboard, thus raising them from the wall and creating a raised frame effect.

☞
Preparing the surface,
page 16
Wallpapering, page 66

CREATING A PRINT ROOM
Normally prints are placed between the dado and the ceiling molding. Choose pictures whose theme complements the character of the room. Always make sure that the paint on the walls is dry before gluing on your prints.

YOU WILL NEED
For a print room
Utility knife and new blades
Visual reference: postcards (old and new), art books, old historical prints, home decorating magazines, catalogs
Metal rule
Pencil
Wallpaper paste
2in flat brush
Soft brush

1 | Choose images from magazines, old catalogs, and art history books. If necessary. reduce them to scale using a color photocopier. However. you may not need to do this, as such reproductions are often close to dollhouse scale.

2 | Cut out the pictures using a utility knife and a metal rule. Make sure the blade is sharp; otherwise, the paper will tear. Arrange the prints together to find out which images work best next to each other, before gluing them to the wall one at a time.

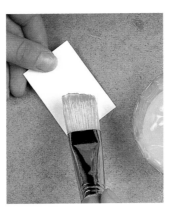

4 | Mix a small quantity of wallpaper paste according to the manufacturer's instructions. Paste both the wall and the back of the paper print.

3 | The spacing between each image needs to be carefully considered. A gap of about ½ to 1 in usually works best, depending on the required look. Pasting the pictures close together will give the impression of a gallery. Measure the spaces with a metal rule and mark lightly in pencil.

6 | An informal feeling is achieved by hanging the pictures at differing heights. The choice of background wallpaper or paint should enhance the colors in the pictures and be in keeping with the theme of the room. Here the fresh green of the painted wall and the lattice wallpaper complement the Japanese-style botanical and bird images.

5 | Place the print on the wall in the marked position and smooth it with a soft brush or the palm of your hand to release any air bubbles or creases.

MAKING PAPER FRAMES

Making paper frames by cutting out pictures from art catalogs is less expensive than buying miniature wooden moldings. Cut out paper frames work in black and white and in color. If you are working with a monochrome original, you can also successfully hand color the frame. This framing technique allows you to be inventive, giving a personal touch to your pictures.

YOU WILL NEED

For paper frames
Catalog pictures or paper
  for framing strip
Scalpel
Metal rule
Cardboard
Pencil
Masking tape
Wallpaper paste
2in flat brush

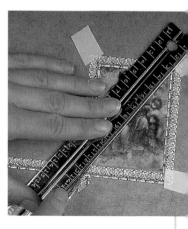

4 | Place the framing strips around the picture and secure with masking tape. Make sure all the measurements are correct then cut your final bottom left angle, taking a diagonal across of 45 degrees which should be in line with the opposite angle, resulting in four lengths square to the picture.

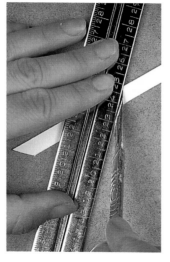

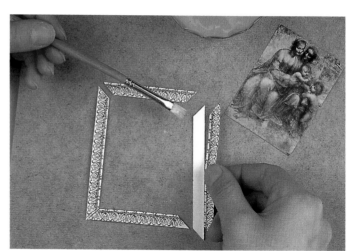

1 | When you have chosen the appropriate framing strip, cut the paper into strips about ¼in wide. Using a sharp scalpel and a metal rule, cut the end of the paper strip at a 45 degree angle to miter the corners.

2 | If you want a three-dimensional frame, cut out strips of thin cardboard the same size as the paper strips with a scalpel.

3 | Place the paper strips on to the cardboard strips, mark the position with a pencil then cut at a 45 degree angle. Make sure your scalpel is sharp so as not to tear the card.

5 | Finally glue your four lengths to the raised cardboard with a small amount of wallpaper paste. When the paste is dry stick your picture onto the wall and glue the four corners around it creating the illusion of a real frame. The other option is to cut out a rectangle piece of cardboard including the measurements of both the image and the frame and mount onto the card, when dry stick the joined picture and frame onto the wall.

Stenciling

USING STENCILS ON YOUR

DOLLHOUSE WALLS AND FURNISHINGS

CAN CREATE PLEASING RESULTS. THE

TECHNIQUE PROVIDES AN EFFECTIVE WAY OF

CREATING SIMPLE REPEAT PATTERNS.

Stencils have been used to decorate wallpaper, walls, and furnishings in Europe since the 17th century. The stencil device originated in China and has been used by the Chinese since 3000 B.C. Stenciling in various forms has been used to decorate dollhouses since the early Bavarian-style houses. Stencils were mainly used to decorate façades, furnishings, and walls, and it is a good technique for creating fairly accurate, handpainted repeat patterns, such as decorative borders above or below a dado and on furniture.

A stencil works as a mask, covering areas which must not be printed or painted, thus creating a positive image from a cutout shape. Stencils can be made from various materials, such as thin cardboard or plastic. When using stencils to decorate your dollhouse, remember to stick to a scale of 1:12, which means that your stencil motif should not be any bigger than 1in. You will soon notice if you do go out of scale; the design will not fit comfortably with the scale of the architecture and furnishings.

MATERIALS Always use a sharp utility knife to score and cut out the stencil pattern; accuracy is essential to achieve a neat, well-defined outline. Aim to keep your pattern simple but effective within the style of the room. Use spray paint or a stencil brush to apply the pattern. For stenciling walls, it is best to print your stencil on thin cardboard or paper, not directly onto the interior of your dollhouse. Work on a flat surface and measure and mark in your design before starting. If you are applying stencils on to furniture, work directly onto the surface, taping the stencil in position first.

☞
Preparing the surface,
page 16
Blocking designs, page 27

STENCILING A PIECE OF FURNITURE

Here a ready-cut stencil made of copper is used to apply a design directly onto a piece of furniture. Such stencils are durable and can be used again and again. Prime and sand the surface of the furniture before painting and applying the stencil.

YOU WILL NEED
For furniture
1in and ½in brush
Copper stencil
Wet and dry sandpaper
Stencil brush
Masking tape
Acrylic paint
Gold powder paint

1 | Paint the piece of furniture with two coats of acrylic paint. When the paint is completely dry, sand with wet and dry paper until the surface is completely smooth.

2 | Use a fine brush to paint into the intricate areas, and sand when it is dry.

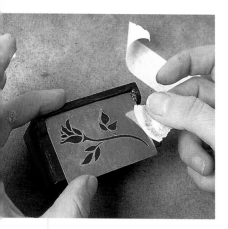

3 | Place the copper stencil in position and secure it firmly with masking tape, keeping it flat to the surface.

5 | Once the paint is dry, peel off the tape holding the stencil in place.

4 | Mix the paint for the stencil fairly thickly and apply it with a stencil brush. Try to keep the stencil still when applying the paint; otherwise, the image will have blurred edges.

6 | Remove the stencil, and wipe off any excess paint from the edges. Apply further stenciled images until you have achieved the desired effect.

7 | The ultramarine blue of the finished piece contrasts strikingly with the gold paint of the stencil. If you require a gloss finish, the piece can be varnished with acrylic gloss varnish or French polish.

MAKING A STENCIL USING A HOLE PUNCH

The hole punch technique allows you to make a stencil of a repeated dot pattern which can be applied to paper to make your own dotted wallpaper. You can also create a decorative border pattern below the molding or on a piece of furniture.

YOU WILL NEED
Repeat pattern stencils
Hole punch
Acetate sheet
Metal rule
Masking tape
Stencil brush
Damp cloth
Paper

1 | Using a hole punch, make evenly spaced holes in a sheet of stencil acetate. Use a grid cutting mat as a guide or a metal rule to measure the distance between the holes.

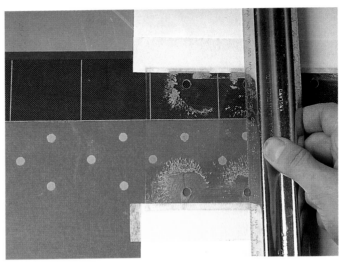

2 | Place the stencil on the surface to be decorated. In this case the stencil is being printed on paper. Secure the stencil in position with masking tape. Apply paint with a stencil brush, starting at the top edge of the paper.

5 | Use a metal rule to check the spacing of the dots. Continue to work down the paper until your design is complete.

3 | When the first row is complete, remove the stencil and clean it using a damp cloth.

4 | Reposition the stencil further down the paper. Stick a piece of scrap paper onto the top edge of the acetate to keep the paper on which you are working clean.

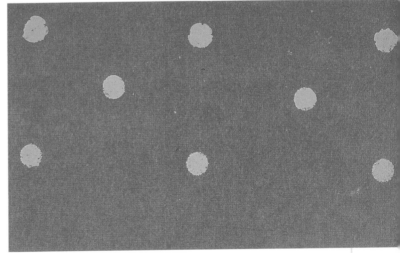

6 | The finished paper can be glued onto a wall or can be cut into strips to create a patterned border.

STENCILING A DECORATIVE BORDER

The image for your stencil should be a simple shape; otherwise, it will be too complicated to be cut out. You can either draw your own design or copy an image from a magazine or other visual reference. Choose a design that is in an appropriate scale for the room. You may need to reduce a motif that is too large on a photocopier. In this project a stenciled design is used to create a decorative border in a bathroom.

YOU WILL NEED

For a border
Utility knife
Metal rule
Masking tape
Round stencil brush, small size
Thin smooth plastic stencil acetate sheet
Fiber-tip marker
Small jars of acrylic or latex paint
Wallpaper paste
2in flat brush
Paper or thin cardboard

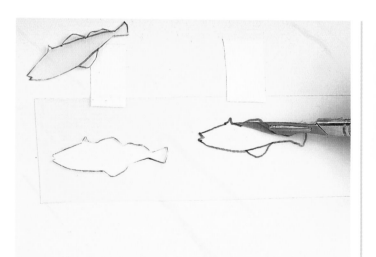

1 | Place your original design on a flat surface and secure the corners with masking tape. Cut out a strip of transparent stencil acetate, place it over the design, and secure with tape. Using a permanent fiber-tip marker, trace the image through the plastic.

2 | You can either trace a single image or you may decide to include two or more repeats of the image on your stencil. If you repeat the design, consider the spacing between each image; you may want to vary the height of the images, as in the example shown. Using a very sharp knife, score the stencil acetate, following the outline. You may have to score around the image several times before achieving a clean cut.

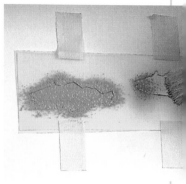

3 | Always print your stencil on thin cardboard or paper, not directly onto the interior of your dollhouse. Cut the cardboard or paper to size before you start. Measure and mark in your design on the paper, considering the spacing between each image or group of images, before applying the color. Mix some acrylic paint to a creamy consistency. Make sure the paint isn't runny. Apply the paint with a stencil brush, dabbing lightly to cover the image completely.

4 | When the paint is nearly dry, lift off the stencil, check the border strip is the length of the wall, then apply wallpaper paste to both the wall and the paper. Trim off any excess paper when the paste is dry. If you attempt to trim while it is still damp it is likely to tear.

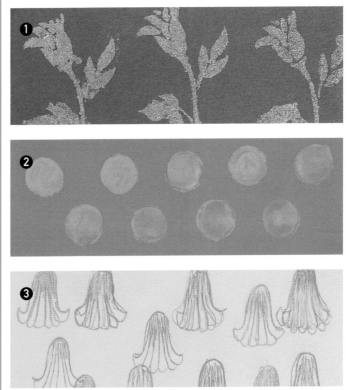

5 | The simplicity of this border design works well in this bathroom setting, reflecting the watery theme. The blue of the fish contrasts pleasingly with the pale yellow background, and harmonizes with the color scheme of the room. The handpainted quality of the stencil gives the room a personal touch, making a refreshing alternative to manufactured wallpapers.

The stenciled examples shown here illustrate the variety of effects obtainable with this versatile technique. You can create formal or informal designs depending on your choice of color and pattern.

❶ Gold powder mixed with denatured alcohol and shellac varnish has been used for the stencil decoration on a painted background of ultramarine mixed with a little cerulean blue. This opulent design would look marvelous as a decorative border.

❷ Ideal for a child's bedroom wallpaper, this hole-punch design derives much of its impact from the use of complementary colors— red and green. For a more restful effect, choose pastels or different shades of the same color.

❸ This informal repeat pattern was created using transfer paper. When you draw over the transfer paper with a pointed instrument such as a pencil, the ink is transferred to the surface below. Designs such as this can be drawn freehand or by using a template or stencil as a guide.

Tiling

WHATEVER STYLE OR PERIOD OF DOLLHOUSE YOU HAVE CHOSEN TO DECORATE, TILING IS BOUND TO BE APPROPRIATE EITHER FOR FLOORS OR WALLS. TO ACHIEVE TILE EFFECTS, YOU CAN USE PATTERNED PAPER, MOLDED FIBER OR PLASTIC SHEET TILES, OR REAL CERAMIC TILES.

Tiles of one sort or another have been in use for centuries. The three main systems to achieve tile effects—patterned paper, molded fiber or plastic sheet tiles, and real ceramic tiles—are complicated to make yourself, so the assumption is that you will buy them.

PATTERNED PAPER Using patterned paper is simple and cost-effective, but it can look a little flat when laid. If you require a gloss finish, you can apply one or more coats of high-gloss clear varnish after you are sure the paper is properly dry. The more coats you apply, the higher the gloss will be.

MOLDED FIBER OR PLASTIC SHEET TILES The molded fiber or plastic sheet tile is more expensive, but it is a finished product, with no need for varnishing. These products are quite simple to apply to your floor using a multipurpose glue (not white craft glue). When cutting the molded sheets, first cut a template of cardboard or thick paper, and make sure that it fits snugly in the room. Using the template as a guide, cut the sheet with a utility knife, using a good blade. Cut accurately; mistakes can be costly.

CERAMIC TILES Your third choice is to use ceramic tiles. These are the most expensive of all and the most difficult to lay, because they are not easy to cut. You need to use tile pliers to cut ceramic tiles. The ceramics come on a backing sheet normally made from nylon mesh. Again, make a template using cardboard and glue the tiles to it using multipurpose glue. When you are shopping for your tiles, it is a good idea to take your template to the store, as many

"workshop stores" will be able to cut the tiles for you if you don't have tile pliers. The gaps between the tiles should be grouted, using standard tile grout in accordance with the manufacturer's instructions. When you are satisfied that the tiling looks properly finished, simply lay the template with tiles attached on the floor, or lightly glue it in place using the same glue as before. If you are tiling walls, perhaps in the kitchen or bathroom, the method is the same, but you may need to support the sheet because of the weight of the ceramics. Use masking tape to stick the top edge in position, and lean weights such as food cans against the walls.

> **TIPS OF THE TRADE**
> Flowers or other small objects can be cut from miniature wallpaper and glued on plain tiles to give a handpainted effect.

TILING

The introduction of tiled floors and/or walls into any dollhouse will add to the decorative impact. Choosing the right tiles for your period is important, so do some research first. Placing 20th-century tiles in, say, a Georgian townhouse would be a mistake that would undermine the authentic effect. It is best to leave the tiling until all other decoration is complete, as paint splashes may be difficult to remove.

1 │ Here, terracotta ceramic floor tiles have been selected. These are purchased in sheets mounted on a nylon or similar mesh backing.

YOU WILL NEED
For tiling
Sheets of tiles
Grout (powder)
Tile cutter
Utility knife
Cardboard
Pliers
Multipurpose glue
Brush
Spreader
Cloth

2 | Mix the grout according to the manufacturer's instructions, and leave it to stand for 20 to 30 minutes. Make sure it is not too runny and that there are no lumps left in the mix, as these can cause problems when you do the grouting.

4 | Apply multipurpose glue to the mesh and use a brush to spread it evenly, making sure no glue gets on the edges of the tiles. Do not apply glue too thickly as it can ooze through the mesh and get on the surface.

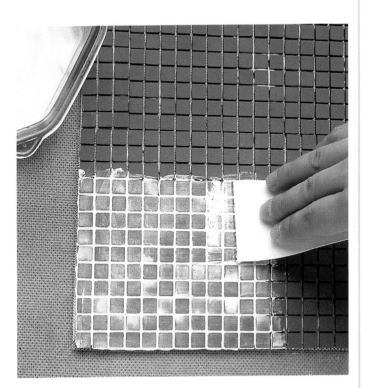

3 | Cut a piece of cardboard or thick paper to the exact size of the floor/wall. Place the sheets of tiles on this backing to determine how many you will need and how they will need to be trimmed to cover the floor area. Turn any sheets that need to be trimmed face down and cut between lines using a utility knife. Use a tile cutter and pair of pliers to cut through individual tiles.

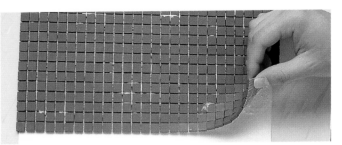

5 | Apply the glued sheet of tiles onto the cardboard and flatten out carefully. Check that the rows of tiles have not closed up or moved out of their straight lines. If they have, open the joints with your knife blade and straighten.

6 | Apply the grout with a spreader (a piece of flexible plastic or thick cardboard works well), pressing down into the gaps. Be sure there are no air pockets or gaps in the grouting.

7 | When the grouting is complete, remove any excess from the surface with a damp cloth. Apply even pressure to give even coverage over the whole floor area.

8 | When dry, polish off any grout residue with a dry cloth. Fully glazed tiles are easier to clean than semi-glazed ones.

TIPS OF THE TRADE
If a whole tile will not fit to suit an opening in a doorway, say, or around a fireplace, it can be cut using a pair of pliers and a pair of tile pliers.

WALL TILING
Molded fiber or plastic sheets of tiles are commonly used on walls, but can also be laid on floors. The method is the same for both. These tiles can be expensive, so where measuring is awkward, use a cardboard template and check before transferring the measurements to the tile sheet.

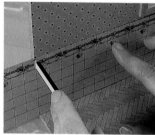

YOU WILL NEED
For wall tiling
Sheets of tiles
Pencil for marking
Utility knife
Ruler
Sandpaper
Multipurpose or white
  craft glue
Masking tape

1 | Hold the tile sheet against the wall and mark the position of the cut on the right side of the sheet.

2 | Most of this type of sheet tiling can be snapped at the joints, if, however, the type that you are using cannot, or if you need to cut through a tile to achieve a precise fit, you will need to use a utility knife. Be sure to use a new blade and apply only slight pressure. Use a ruler as a guide.

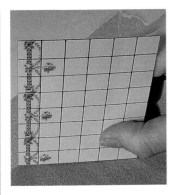

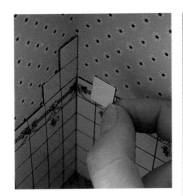

3 | When the section of tiling is cut to length and height, smooth the cut ends by placing a sheet of medium-grit sandpaper on the workbench, and rubbing back and forth. Check after each stroke.

5 | Single tiles can be used to make patterns behind stoves, sinks, and bathtubs. If you want to stick tiles on wallpaper, use only solvent-based glue. Water-based glues may loosen the paper.

4 | Check that the tiling fits perfectly and when satisfied, glue into place using a multipurpose glue or white craft glue. If the sheets are tending to bend away from the wall, secure with masking tape at the top and place a weight halfway down the wall to keep the tiling in place until the glue has dried.

Like some other finishes for dollhouse interiors, real ceramic tiles can be costly, and not all budgets will run to such expense. The tile-effect papers shown here offer an alternative. Dollhouse suppliers usually stock a wide range of colors and designs.

❶ and ❷ A design of large square tiles with contrasting corner inserts is shown in two different color schemes. This pattern is perfect for a bathroom or kitchen floor. Choose a color combination to suit your overall color scheme.

❸ This design of small tiles and corner inserts would work well on bathroom walls as well as on floors.

❹ Blue and white is a traditional combination of colors for tiles, used all over the world. Consider this for a bathroom floor with plain white fixtures or behind a sink in a country-style kitchen.

❺ A further variation on the blue and white theme, this interesting pattern would be great for a kitchen floor.

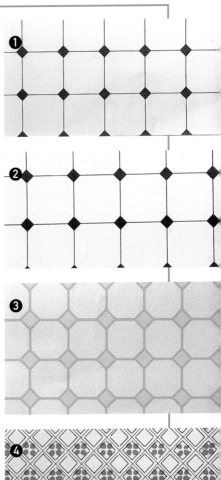

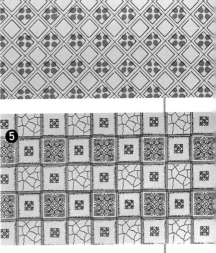

Varnishing

VARNISH PROTECTS AND SEALS A PAINTED SURFACE AND ADDS DEPTH AND SHEEN TO A DECORATED FINISH. THERE ARE SEVERAL TYPES AND FINISHES OF VARNISH AVAILABLE, ALLOWING YOU PLENTY OF CHOICE WHEN VARNISHING FLOORS OR PAINTED SURFACES IN YOUR DOLLHOUSE.

There are many varnishes available, and it is essential to select the right varnish for the job you are working on. There are two distinct types of varnish—oil-based and water-based. Oil-based varnish is used on an oil-based surface, such as faux marble, while water-based varnish is used on a water-based surface, such as acrylic paint or watercolor. Never apply a water-based varnish to an oil-based surface, as they are not compatible.

TYPES OF FINISH Oil-based polyurethane is a good all-round varnish, and this gives a hard, durable finish. It may lack the character of traditional varnishes, yet several techniques can be applied to enhance the surface at a later stage. Three standard finishes are available: flat, which has almost no shine; satin, which has a semi-gloss finish; and gloss, which has a shiny finish. Varnish is also available ready mixed with various wood stains, imitating different types of wood such as mahogany and oak. You can experiment with these color options to reflect different periods and tastes. With 1:12 scale, imperfections in a varnished surface will be far more noticeable, so aim for as smooth a finish as possible. Several thin coats of varnish are more effective than one thick coat, so you might need to dilute the varnish with mineral spirits or turpentine.

BRUSHES The quality and type of brush is also important; recommended is a soft, flat ½in watercolor brush. Applying varnish with a brush is practical; however, a spray lacquer in aerosol form can work well on a water-based surface.

VARNISHING
Make sure you are in a dust-free room before you start, as wet varnish attracts hair or dust, which can ruin the finish. Wear clothes that are free from wool or fluff, and make sure the room is well lit so you can see the surface of the varnish while you work. The sequence shown on this page has various applications: varnishing a marbled surface; sealing découpage; varnishing flooring surfaces.

YOU WILL NEED
Varnishing
Soft lint-free cloth
Mineral spirits
Varnish
Soft brush

1 | Clean the surface to be varnished. Use a soft cloth dampened with a little mineral spirits. Thin the varnish to a desired consistency. Stir thoroughly, adding a small amount of mineral spirits into the varnish. Add a little at a time, taking care not to overthin the varnish.

2 | Load a clean, soft brush with the varnish. Test the consistency of the varnish on a piece of scrap paper, working the brush over the paper. This removes any air bubbles and loose hairs. Apply the varnish to the prepared surface using even strokes, picking up any excess varnish with each stroke. Keep re-loading the brush as required, but try not to overload it as the varnish may run if applied too thickly. When the varnish is thoroughly dry, apply another coat if needed.

COLOR VARNISHING AND FRENCH POLISHING

Color varnishing adds a richness of color to plain wood while the French polish adds durability of surface and a glossy finish. Apply the colored varnish to unvarnished wood. If the surface is not porous, sand with fine sandpaper.

YOU WILL NEED

For color varnishing and French polishing
Acrylic gloss varnish
1in brush
Transparent acrylic paint
Lint-free cloth
Liquid French polish
Fine sandpaper

2 | When the first coat is dry, apply a thin coat of clear acrylic varnish to seal the surface.

1 | Mix one part acrylic paint with two parts gloss varnish. Choose a color that dries to a transparent finish such as alizarin crimson. Use a 1in brush and paint on the colored varnish in smooth, even brush strokes, working along the grain, covering the front and back of the door.

3 | To add extra shine and durability, rub in a little French polish using a lint-free cloth. Rub in the polish using a circular motion.

4 | When the polish is completely dry, sand it with fine sandpaper.

5 | Apply further layers of French polish until the desired sheen is achieved. The French polish gives a warm tone and high gloss to the door. The reddish-brown door has been given extra sheen by the application of French polish. It would provide a fitting complement to a turn-of-the-century interior.

Different interior styles can be evoked by using different colored varnishes.

❶ Created using burnt umber, dark ultramarine blue and a small amount of acrylic matt varnish. Good for dark Jacobean interiors.

❷ A medium oak finish is created by mixing burnt raw sienna and acrylic cedar wood satin varnish. Good for interior paneling.

❸ This teak effect is created using raw sienna cedar wood acrylic varnish. Works well with gold leaf and baroque interiors.

Wallpapers: handmade

HANDMADE WALLPAPERS WORK WELL IN A QUEEN ANNE OR FRENCH BAROQUE-STYLE DOLLHOUSE, OR EVEN IN A 19TH-CENTURY NEW YORK TOWNHOUSE. THESE PERIOD HOUSES WERE VERY DECORATIVE, WHICH GIVES YOU A LOT OF FREEDOM TO USE YOUR IMAGINATION AND TAKE ADVANTAGE OF THIS ORNATE TRADITION.

Handmade wallpapers have existed in various styles since the 15th century in Europe and even earlier in China. Many early Victorian dollhouses have emulated these styles, which were highly influenced by oriental designs and paintings. Such wallpapers decorated the homes of royalty and the wealthy. Handmade flock papers were also popular; these were made by gluing wool fibers to a printed design to give it a fabric quality. Other wallpaper effects were achieved by joining woodblock prints together and then handpainting them. These styles of wallpaper would be suitable for a Regency or Queen Anne-style dollhouse.

In the 19th century, most wallpapers were machine-printed with serial patterns like those designed and manufactured by William Morris and Art Nouveau designers. These styles of wallpaper would be suitable for a Georgian or Victorian townhouse. This section covers short-cut techniques to help you achieve these historical styles of wallpaper, the first being how to make reduced-to-scale wallpapers.

☞
Wallpapering, page 66

MAKING REDUCED-TO-SCALE WALLPAPERS

Reduced-to-scale wallpaper can be made from reproductions and photocopies reduced to an appropriate scale. If possible, use a color photocopier with a repeat facility. You need to take into account that a large image will need to be reduced considerably more than a small repeat pattern. It is always advisable to take a piece of commercial dollhouse paper with you when you are photocopying so that you can check the accuracy of the scale. The best way to judge is by eye. Select a design or pattern that you think will photocopy well. One with a contrasting range of tones is best.

1 | Here a large image has been selected. If you do not want to cut the reproduction out of the book or magazine, you can always photocopy the original. To reduce an image to one twelfth of the original size, carry out the following stage-by-stage reduction: reduce the image by 50 percent three times, then do a final reduction of 75 percent. Copy the final image four or five times depending on the format or type of pattern. Then cut out the images and glue them on a sheet of photocopy paper.

2 | Choose the desired color on the color photocopier and press repeat. If the photocopier you are using doesn't have a repeat facility, you will need to cut and paste the reduced images manually to obtain a sheet of "wallpaper."

4 | Apply handmade paper to the walls in the same way as commercial paper (see p.66).

5 | In this example, handmade wallpaper is used in conjunction with varnished wooden paneling (see Paneling, p.70). The effect, reinforced by the furniture and other decorative details, is that of a 17th-century interior.

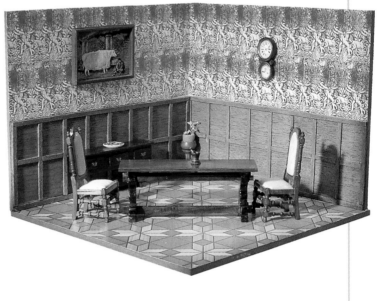

3 | The photocopied sheet will consist of horizontal panels of a repeating pattern. If you do not want the small gaps between the rows, cut out the panels and glue them on another piece of paper with the images joined and copy again.

MAKING FLOCK WALLPAPER

This technique emulates the early handmade wallpapers which had a textured fabric finish. Here loose fibers are glued onto preprinted papers. Flock fibers can be bought from model-making suppliers. This style of wallpaper was very popular in Regency and early Georgian houses, and works well with varnished wooden panels and added architectural decoration.

YOU WILL NEED
Flock wallpapers
Flock fibers
Preprinted paper
Fine paintbrush
White craft glue
Strainer

1 | Select a preprinted paper of the correct scale. Make sure it is of a suitable design. Here a bold floral repeating design with an ornate linking pattern has been chosen. Make sure the colors of the paper work in combination with the color of the loose flock.

2 | Using a fine-pointed brush, paint white craft glue onto the areas to which you want to stick the flock. Work in sections so that the glue remains sticky and the flock sticks firmly to the surface.

3 | Put the loose flock into a small strainer and shake it gently to sprinkle the flock onto the glued area.

4 | Continue to sprinkle on the flock until you have built up a thick layer over the surface.

5 | Shake off the excess flock before allowing the glue to dry. This takes about ten minutes.

6 | To build up a dense covering of flock, apply more glue to the areas you have already worked and add more flock. Work in sections as before.

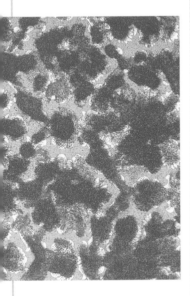

7 | This rich red flock paper would give a warm, ornate feel to a grand room. The paper can be used in conjunction with a dado, wooden paneling, or architectural details.

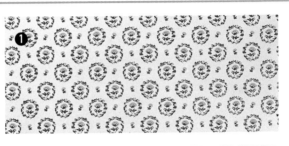

Wallpapers, whether you make them yourself or choose to use preprinted sheets from your dollhouse supplier, are one of the chief means of giving a room character. Here, floral and geometric designs give an indication of the range of effects that are possible.

❶ This rose garland motif wallpaper is based on a 19th-century American design. Its simplicity and freshness make it an ideal choice for a bedroom, where it would complement pink or pale blue woodwork.

❷ This diamond repeat pattern with its floral vine motif would be suitable for a living room or main hallway. It works well above a dado with a plain wallpaper or paintwork below. Teak varnished floorboards or furniture would pick up the touches of orange in the design.

❸ Suitable for a kitchen, this strong floral design has a fresh feel that could be used in combination with a plain tiled floor or pastel green paper.

❹ Arts and Crafts style wallpaper provides instant period character. With its combination of yellows and browns this example would provide a superb complement to rich-brown wooden furniture. It could be used in conjunction with wood paneling in a Victorian-style living room.

❺ Too busy to use over an entire room, this bold daisy pattern could be used above a dado with plain walls below. It would provide a wonderful accent of pattern and color in any large room.

❻ This blue and white Regency stripe has an elegance that would work well in a formal dining room or study. It could also be used in a less formal setting above a dado.

Wallpapers: hanging

THE TYPE OF WALLPAPER SUITABLE FOR YOUR DOLLHOUSE WILL BE DETERMINED BY ITS ARCHITECTURAL STYLE. HOWEVER, MANY DOLLHOUSES DECORATED TODAY DO NOT STICK RELIGIOUSLY TO ONE TYPE OF DECORATIVE STYLE, BUT REFLECT CONTEMPORARY LIVING AS WELL AS HISTORICAL STYLE.

Dollhouses began to be decorated by the mighty and the humble in Europe in about 1564, covering a wide variety of styles and approaches. Preprinted wallpapers reflecting some of these different styles are available from various retail outlets such as dollhouse suppliers, miniature specialists, modelmaking stores, some toy stores, and various department stores. If you are a beginner, you may need to work from photographs or other visuals, so that you have a definite idea of the style and look you want to achieve.

BEFORE WALLPAPERING Before you start wallpapering, make sure that all the interior handpainting is finished and completely dry. If you try to paint after wallpapering, you will end up with a disaster on your hands, giving yourself a lot of extra work trying to clean up paint drips and apply wallpaper that will not stick to the wet walls. If you wish to have lighting in any of the rooms, make sure that the wiring is complete and securely in place, running across the center of the ceiling and out of the back of the house, before decorating. The wires will eventually be attached to a transformer and power supply. All light fixture connection points must be accessible, so do not wallpaper over them or clog them up with paint or glue. A trick of the trade is to cover light fixtures with a piece of masking tape while decorating, and then remove this when all the painting and wallpapering is finished. All dado, baseboards, and wooden paneling should be applied after the decorating is finished and the walls are dry.

PANORAMIC SCENIC WALLPAPERS Panoramic scenic wallpapering is a grand style of wallpapering, which works well in a dining room or entrance hallway, especially in a Regency-style dollhouse. This theatrical style of wallpaper gives the effect of a handpainted mural. Traditional themes for this wallpaper include tropical landscapes, mythological scenes, and botanical subjects. This type of interior decorating always generates interest from dollhouse enthusiasts because of its historical subject matter and miniature style.

☞

Wallpapers: handmade, page 62
Preparing the surface, page 16
Pillaring, page 88
Trompe l'oeil, page 38
Faux marbling, page 42

YOU WILL NEED
For simple wallpapering
Utility knife
Extra blades
Antifungal wallpaper paste
1in paintbrush
2in paintbrush
Metal rule
Pencil

WALLPAPERING
Papering is time-consuming, but the effect is worth the effort. Patience and a bit of practice with the correct tools are all that's required. The most important tool is a good-quality utility knife and sharp blade. Change the blades regularly. Do not attempt to cut the wallpaper with a blunt blade as this often results in dragging and tearing.

1 | Start with the back wall. Hold the paper flush to the edge where the top of the wall meets the ceiling. Measure from floor to ceiling, allowing an extra inch at the sides and bottom, which will eventually be trimmed off when the paper is dry. Using the metal rule and a pencil, mark the vertical and horizontal measurements, using the pattern of the paper as a guide.

2 | Trim the paper to the marked dimensions with the utility knife and the metal rule.

4 | When you place the paper on the wall, start from the top left. Line up the paper with the top of the wall where it meets the ceiling. Use the palm of your hand to press the paper onto the wall, smoothing away any air bubbles. Continue until you reach the bottom. If you intend to attach baseboard or cornicing, leave that part of the wall unpapered, as the wooden strips adhere better to bare walls.

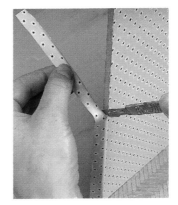

5 | When the paste is completely dry, remove excess paper along the sides and base of the wall with a sharp utility knife. If you try to do this while the paper is still damp, there is a risk that you will tear the paper.

3 | Mix up a small quantity of anti-fungal wallpaper paste. Apply paste evenly to the wall and the back of the paper. It is important to cover both the walls and the paper to prevent the paper from wrinkling, which can ruin the final finish of the house. It may be helpful to add a little water-based colored paint to the paste so that you can see any areas you may have missed.

6 | The finished room has a traditional feel that is further enhanced by the antique-style furniture chosen.

PANORAMIC WALLPAPER

Choose a theme appropriate to the style of your house. This grand panorama of an English stately home in its grounds was taken from a magazine, cut out, and joined together with tape, then duplicated on a color photocopier. If the original is a bit dull, the colors can be slightly enhanced on the copier. Stretch the image on a piece of board (see Stretching paper, p.44) to prevent wrinkles from forming when you apply the acrylic varnish.

YOU WILL NEED
For panoramic scenic wallpaper
Utility knife and new blades
Visual reference: wrapping paper, art books, old prints, photographs
Metal rule
Wallpaper paste
Gummed paper tape
Acrylic paints
Acrylic matt medium
Acrylic gloss varnish
Pasting brush
Selection of nylon paintbrushes
Clean, flat board for stretching paper
Typing paper
White craft glue

1 | Some areas of the image may need handpainting to cover up imperfections, to add surface texture, or to enhance richness of color. Apply acrylic paint with a fine brush. If the paint looks too thick, mix it with acrylic matt medium to extend and dilute the paint, while still maintaining color saturation. You can remove excess paint by blotting with thin newsprint or newspaper.

2 | When any handpainting is dry, seal the image with two coats of acrylic gloss varnish. Let the first coat dry thoroughly before applying the second. The varnish protects the surface and prevents the photocopy from fading over time. The sheen of the gloss finish gives the impression of a highly varnished oil painting.

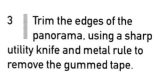

3 | Trim the edges of the panorama, using a sharp utility knife and metal rule to remove the gummed tape.

4 | Measure the room from floor to ceiling, and trim the image as if it were wallpaper (see page 66). If there is a door frame to consider, cut out the frame after the panoramic wallpaper has been pasted on the wall and dried.

9 | Apply white craft glue or wallpaper paste to the reverse side and smooth it with your fingertips to remove creases or air bubbles.

5 | Before applying the painting to the walls, make sure that the continuation of the scene looks convincing and gives the impression of a panoramic theme. Paste both the wall and the back of the paper and place the image on the walls. The ½in gap at the bottom has been left because the baseboard will cover this area. The two sections of paper meet at the doorway where the seam will be least visible.

7 | When the paper is dry, cut out the doorway and trim excess paper with a sharp utility knife.

10 | The finished room looks grand and ornate.

6 | You may have to touch up the painting once it has been stuck to the wall. Here the sky was re-painted to conceal the seam.

8 | This style of wallpapering can be enhanced by further decorative details such as découpage and marble panels and floors. The decorative door pediment is taken from a book of architectural ornament. Cut out your chosen design with a sharp utility knife. If you want to add color, use acrylic paints thinned with matt medium and build up the color in thin layers using a ½in brush.

Wood paneling

WOOD PANELING IS A TECHNIQUE OF DECORATING WALLS AND CEILINGS WITH STRIPS OF WOOD. THESE CAN THEN BE STAINED AND VARNISHED TO SUIT THE ROOM.

Paneling dates from classical architecture as far back as Greek and Roman times, and was a feature of the transitional Italian Romanesque interiors. Its extensive use on walls and ceilings, however, began in the Gothic period. Decorative paneling consists of wide, thin sheets of wood, framed together by narrower, thicker strips, both vertical (styles) and horizontal (rails). Almost always in historical times, paneling was made of oak or pine. In the 20th century, however, a wide variety of woods were used, including walnut, mahogany, birch, and redwood. Fine examples can be seen at Hampton Court Palace near London, and in many buildings dating back to the 17th century in New England.

CHOOSING MATERIALS For the purposes of decorating dollhouses, birch plywood is recommended, as it has a very fine grain and is almost white in color, thereby taking stains of various shades easily. Choose your birch carefully, making sure it is free from knots or any signs of discoloration. For styles and rails check again for quality. Plywood should be ¹⁄₁₆in thick; styles and rails will vary, but as a guide ⅛in will work in most cases.

There is no set size for paneling, it is purely a matter of choice. You can divide a wall in half with just one rail or into three using two rails and so on. How many styles you use will depend upon the size of panels you require.

When you have completed the paneling, you can apply wood stain to finish. Too dark a stain might "close in" the room, so a lighter color might work better. Finally, apply one or more coats of varnish.

☞
Varnishing, page 60

PANELING

Before you start to make the panels, it is a good idea to draw your design on a piece of paper or cardboard and place it in the room to make sure the effect is what you want. First cut out from ¹⁄₁₆-in plywood a backing sheet of the depth of the area to be paneled. Do not trim to the length yet. When the backing is cut to size, first glue all the outside strips, like a picture frame. If you cut a panel too short, discard it and cut another rather than trying to "make do." The cost of such small strips is negligible, and you can use these scraps to test your finishing color. When gluing, be sure not to leave any glue on the face of the panels; wipe it off with a damp cloth immediately.

YOU WILL NEED
For paneling
Birch plywood
Square
Pencil
Utility knife
Glue (craft) PVA
Adhesive tape
Wood stain
Brush for stain
Brush for varnish
Flat or gloss varnish

1 | Hold the backing piece against the wall, making sure that you allow for the panel on the adjoining wall. Mark the vertical edge carefully with a square, allowing the thickness of the pencil line to be cut off.

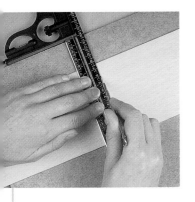

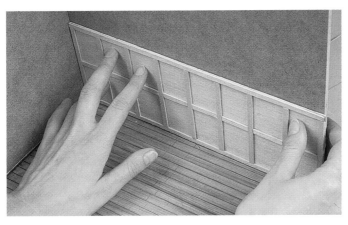

2 | On a work board, cut just inside the marked line using a utility knife or fine-tooth razor saw. Then check the fit of the backing on the wall. If the backing is a fraction short, don't worry, you can compensate by gluing the first strip slightly higher than the edge.

4 | When one panel is made, place it in position using tape, and measure the next backing piece, having butted the end to the finished panel. Complete the panel as before.

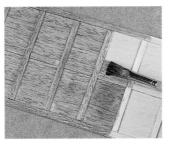

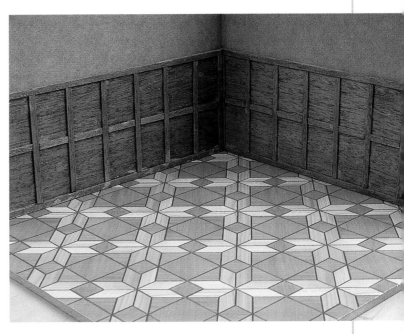

3 | Cut out strips of plywood for the two vertical and two horizontal edges of the panel. Proceed to cut shorter lengths of plywood for the verticals (styles) and the horizontals (rails). Although you don't want large spaces between the strips, small gaps can add to the authentic effect as old panel often has shrinkage gaps at the joints.

5 | When all the required panels are complete, test your chosen wood stain on some scraps of plywood (more than one color test is a good idea). Having made your choice of color, stain the panels lightly at first. Add a little more stain if the results are not dark enough. Wait for the stain to dry and finish in flat or gloss varnish. When all the panels are complete, glue in position on the walls of the room.

6 | Try to choose a floor finish that will complement the color and effect of the paneled room. Here a geometric tiled floor in shades of brown reinforces the Jacobean effect of the paneling.

Floors
and
Carpets

Carpeting

LAYING CARPET IN YOUR DOLLHOUSE WILL ENHANCE THE FINISHED LOOK OF ANY ROOM. AS WITH OTHER DECORATING TECHNIQUES, CAREFUL AND PRECISE MEASURING MAKES ALL THE DIFFERENCE TO THE RESULT.

There are many types of carpet on the market, from simple plain felt, to hand-knotted, multicolored, multipatterned carpet, the latter being very expensive and out of reach for most of us. You may, however, find suitable scraps of material or felt in the remnants box at your local store. Choosing carpet is important. The right carpet in the wrong room of your dollhouse—and vice versa, could be a minor disaster. Generally, your eye will tell you —if it looks right, then it probably *is* right. You can always do some homework, to achieve the correct color and/or pattern of carpet for your period and style of house.

MEASURING AND CUTTING When measuring your carpet, be sure to allow for the thickness of baseboards, if they are to be used. Measure the width and depth of your room carefully; cutting too large a piece will result in bulges, while cutting too small a piece will leave gaps around the walls. Cut your carpet using a utility knife with a new blade, applying firm pressure on your metal rule. This should give a clean cut and avoid frayed edges.

LAYING When laying the carpet, you have two choices: you can glue your carpet using a contact glue (white craft glue may ooze through the weave) or stick it down using double-sided tape. The tape method is recommended, since the carpet is then easily removed for cleaning or replacing. Your carpet probably will not get too dirty, but any light marks should be wiped off using household carpet cleaner. Using real carpet rarely works well as it is generally far too thick and your miniature furniture won't stand properly. Many carpet stores have pattern books with swatches, and these are sometimes very thin. You may be able to obtain some samples that are no longer needed.

CHOOSING CARPETS AND RUGS

When deciding on carpet or rugs for your rooms, consider the decor of each room carefully, and think of what type of furnishings are to be used. Period is important; a jazzy 1960s carpet in a colonial setting, for example, would be a mistake. There are, of course, no rules as to what you may or may not use, but to get an authentic "feel," you need to do some research. Rugs also can play an important part in finishing the setting. These can be bought in various sizes, colors, and patterns. They range from a simple and inexpensive printed pattern to costly handwoven examples. If you are good with a needle, you could even make your own using very fine-gauge canvas and thread.

YOU WILL NEED
Laying carpets
Utility knife
Marking pen
Metal rule
Glue or double-sided tape
Weights
Piece of plywood

1 If you are making wall-to-wall carpets, measuring is all important. It is a good idea to make a paper template and test this in the room, making sure it lies perfectly flat on the floor.

2 When you are confident that your measurements are correct, transfer them to your carpet, using a marking pen that shows clearly. Always check that your marks are clearly visible before you start to cut.

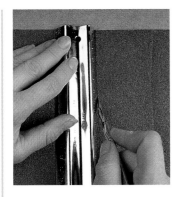

5 | Be sure that the floor is clean and free from dust. Carefully lay the carpet in place, smoothing out any ridges with the palm of your hand. Take care not to use excessive pressure that could stretch the carpet. Lay a piece of board slightly smaller than the room on top of the carpet. Place a weight on it and leave it for several hours.

3 | Using a metal rule and a utility knife with a new blade, cut the carpet to the marks. Be sure not to cut it too small. It is better to cut the carpet a little too large as you can always trim it afterward. Use firm pressure on the blade to be sure of cutting in one stroke to avoid fraying. Check the fit of the carpet in the room and trim if necessary.

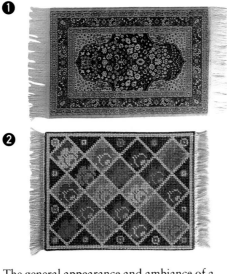

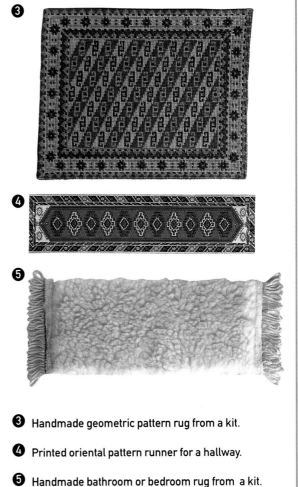

The general appearance and ambiance of a room can be greatly altered by furnishings. One of the best ways to get that warm lived-in look is with carefully selected rugs. You can make your own rugs from inexpensive kits bought from your local dollhouse supplier or you can buy them ready made. Ready-made rugs range from cheap printed designs on cotton to expensive hand-knotted rugs in pure silk.

❶ Printed oriental pattern rug.

❷ Handmade rose design rug from a kit.

❸ Handmade geometric pattern rug from a kit.

❹ Printed oriental pattern runner for a hallway.

❺ Handmade bathroom or bedroom rug from a kit.

4 | Depending upon the type of carpet used, apply double-sided tape to the edges or apply a little contact glue, or if you are using self-adhesive type, peel off the backing.

Flooring

THE FLOORING IN A DOLLHOUSE IS VERY IMPORTANT AS IT IS THE FIRST THING TO CATCH YOUR EYE AS YOU LOOK INSIDE. THERE ARE MANY WAYS TO FINISH THE FLOORS, INCLUDING USING REAL FLOORBOARDS, PAINTED EFFECTS, AND TILING.

The most effective method to finish floors is to use real floorboards, which you can make yourself by cutting very thin birch plywood into strips. Alternatively, you can buy thin strips of hardwood from most hobby stores or miniatures suppliers. Making floorboards is time-consuming but quite simple, especially if you use bought materials. You simply glue the strips of wood in place using white craft wood glue, then sandpaper lightly, and finish in your chosen color of paint or varnish. You can also achieve a good board effect by cutting a sheet of thin birch plywood to the size of your floor, and scoring lines in the face using a hooked blade, then finish as before. Another simpler method is to draw the lines on the floor itself using a pencil, then finish with slightly colored varnish. Test the color of the varnish on a sample piece of similar surface.

If you would like to make real floorboards but find the cost prohibitive, try asking your local coffee bar to save discarded stirring sticks; these make fine floorboards after the round ends have been cut off! To finish the floor, use solvent-based paint or varnish, as the water-based type may cause the boards to lift or buckle.

Many floor finishes printed on wallpaper are available: These include black and white tiles, parquet, boards, Italian marble tiles, and quarry tiles. Another good flooring effect is to paint a border around the edges of the room using a stencil or printing block and contrasting color print prior to the finishing coat of varnish.

☞ Varnishing, page 60

"REAL" FLOORBOARDS
Decide on the decor of your room before making up your mind about the floor. Black and white tiles look good in hallways, while varnished floorboards look wonderful in both period style and modern living rooms.

YOU WILL NEED
For real floorboards
Birch plywood or hardwood strips
Ruler
Utility knife
Miter block
Fine and medium-grit sandpaper
White craft glue
Damp cloth
Brushes
Wood stain or paint
Clear varnish

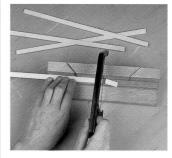

1 | Carefully measure the length of your floorboards, making sure that they fit easily into the room. Cut them a little shorter than the measured length to allow for any expansion due to moisture. If they are too tight, they will swell up and buckle. Use a miter block to cut the ends square.

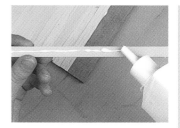

2 | Make sure that the floor of the dollhouse is free from dust, and smooth any paint "pimples" by sanding lightly. Apply a small amount of white craft glue along the center of a floorboard and lay the board in place. Wipe off any glue that oozes out from under the board with a damp cloth.

3 | When all the boards have been glued in place, lay a piece of board the same size as the floor on top of the boards with a weight on top and leave overnight; the boards should be firmly stuck and flat. For a perfectly smooth finish, sand with a medium-grit sandpaper, following the grain of the boards. Test the color of stain or paint you require on a piece of scrap floorboard. One coat of stain is generally all that is needed. Finish with a coat of clear varnish (see p.60). For a high gloss, use more than one coat, sanding with very fine sandpaper between coats.

DRAWN FLOORBOARDS

This method of achieving "floorboards" is simple and cheap. If done carefully and with forethought, it can also be very effective. Choose a base color that resembles the type of wood you are aiming to recreate: use a reddish brown for a mahogany floor, dark brown for dark oak, or a pale yellow for an antique pine (as shown). Finish with a coat of a colored varnish.

YOU WILL NEED

For drawn floorboards
Masking tape
Flat brush
Base coat
Pencil
Ruler
Flat or gloss varnish
Stain

1 | Test several color variations on a piece of scrap wood of the same type as the floor. If none is available, use the underside of the house for testing. Use masking tape to protect the bottom of the walls before you start. Apply the base color smoothly and evenly with a flat brush. Make sure no patches are left unpainted.

2 | Decide on the width of the "boards" you require; generally ½in or less looks fine. When the paint is completely dry, draw parallel pencil lines with the help of a ruler. If you have used a dark base color, be sure that your lines are dark enough to be visible by using a little pressure. For a truly authentic floorboard effect, draw a few lines across the boards to indicate floorboard ends.

3 | If the base coat has created the color of boards you intend, finish with clear varnish (flat or gloss). If not, mix a little stain into your varnish and test. Varnish the whole floor evenly. Let it dry overnight. To apply further coats of varnish, sand with fine sandpaper between coats.

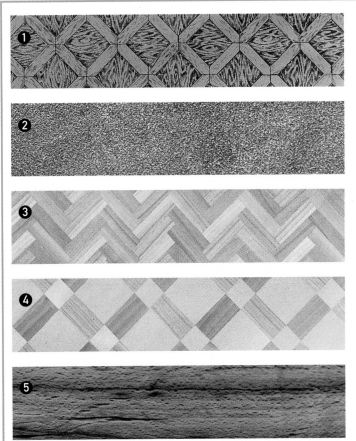

If time and budget are limited, consider floor coverings printed on paper. This is a quick and inexpensive alternative to floorboards, carpets, or real tiles. Several different finishes are shown here.

❶ Linoleum-effect paper for use in a kitchen or bathroom.

❷ This paper simulating marble would be suitable for any grand entrance. It could also provide marble-look table tops in a kitchen or period living room.

❸ Herringbone is a traditional pattern for parquet flooring. It would look particularly appropriate in a study or library, partly covered by rugs.

❹ This diamond pattern parquet could be used in a grand ballroom or entrance hall.

❺ This paper creates the effect of a dark floor boards, suitable for a Jacobean interior. The paper can be glued to the floor in a single sheet or cut into strips to provide a less uniform look.

EXTERIOR

WALLS

Brick façades

BRICKS OF ONE TYPE OR ANOTHER HAVE BEEN IN USE FOR THOUSANDS OF YEARS, SO WHATEVER PERIOD YOU CHOOSE, BRICKWORK WILL NO DOUBT BE IN KEEPING. BRICKS ARE ALSO USED WORLDWIDE, EXCEPT IN REGIONS WHERE THERE IS NO NATIVE CLAY OR BRICK EARTH.

Traditional brickwork can be created with the use of a good quality wood putty, a little white craft glue, some water, paint, and wood stain. Using this three-dimensional or relief effect, you can achieve many different brick façades. The finish or color of the bricks will alter the look of your house completely, so before you begin to color, paint, or stain, do your research to determine what type of brick would have been used in the area and period that your house is coming from. You may also decide that you want your house to look old. If so, follow the step-by-step instructions, then refer to Antiquing (page 24), which will tell you how to achieve an aged effect. This method is time-consuming but inexpensive. It is also quite easy; no special skills are needed other than the ability to paste your wood putty on flat and then mark out lines. The basic tools required are listed.

WOODEN FIBER BRICKWORK Wooden fiber brickwork is quite expensive and also time-consuming, but effective. Sheets of fiber brickwork can be bought from all good dollhouse stores or miniaturist suppliers.

☞

Preparing the surface, page 16
Antiquing, page 24

USING PRINTED PAPER Another method is to use printed paper. This is widely available and comes in many colors. The main advantage of using paper is speed. The method is the same for all types.

YOU WILL NEED
For wooden fiber brickwork
Sheets of brickwork
Spring clip
Pencil
Razor saw or utility knife
White craft glue
Damp cloth
Masking tape
Artist's oil paints
Printer's roller

1 | Place the sheet of wooden fiber brickwork face down with the wall on top. Make sure that the two pieces are held squarely in place. A spring clip or something similar will help to prevent slipping. Mark any doors and windows and the overall size of the wall.

TIPS OF THE TRADE
When using printed paper brick façades, add a little food coloring or powder paint to the wallpaper paste in a similar color to your paper. This will help you to see any spots you have missed.

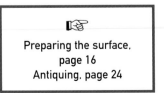

USING WOODEN FIBER BRICKS
This method is expensive but the results are impressive. Measure carefully before you cut the sheets because once a mistake is made it can't be rectified.

2 | When you have marked all openings and dimensions, cut the brickwork sheet to size and cut out the openings using a razor saw or utility knife. If you have a jigsaw, use a fine blade. Repeated strokes with a sharp knife will do just as well.

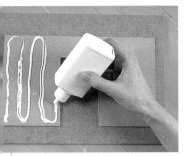

3 | Try the sheet for size, and when you are satisfied, apply white craft glue lightly to the reverse of the brickwork. Make sure that the surface is clean and dust free before applying the glue. Do not use too much glue, as this will make the board soggy and may ooze out when the sheet is placed on the wall.

5 | Choose the color of brickwork you require to match the house style and period. Artist's oil paints are recommended, but any paint can be used. Test the paint on a piece of scrap paper. When you have the correct color, spread a little on a board and roll out with a hard printer's roller (these can be obtained from most art supply stores). Pick up only a light film of paint.

7 | When you have completed the first coat, you can create a more varied effect by mixing a little lighter color into the base color and applying it lightly with the roller. Again, it is best to test first on the piece of scrap you painted earlier. Take care not to add too much of your second color or you will obliterate the base color. Remember you can always add a little more, but you cannot remove any.

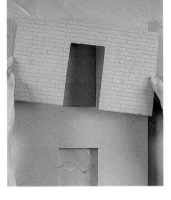

4 | Apply the brickwork to the wall and press down firmly, making sure that the openings on both match exactly. Wipe off any excess glue using a damp cloth. Use masking tape to hold the two layers in place until the glue has dried and set. Cover all the walls in this way.

6 | Test the amount of paint on the roller on a piece of scrap paper before you start. Make sure that the lines between the bricks are not being filled with paint. When the amount of paint on the roller is correct, apply the paint to the brickwork with the roller. Add a little paint at a time.

8 | Complete all the brickwork in this way, slowly building up to the finish you desire. When the paint is dry, hang the windows and doors.

RELIEF BRICKWORK FAÇADE

Your dollhouse will be much admired if you can afford the time and have the patience to create a relief brickwork effect. Other brick finishes can look very good, but none quite matches the effect of a hand-rendered brick façade.

YOU WILL NEED
For relief brickwork façade
Powdered wood putty
White craft glue
Ruler
Plastic spatula
Pointed modeling tool
Medium-grit sandpaper
Fine paintbrush
Paint and wood stain
Masking tape
Old cloth

3 | When all horizontal lines have been scored, begin vertical lines about ¾in apart. Stagger the verticals between alternate rows. Score them freehand to give the bricks a handmade look. Again, brush off excess putty. If you find that the putty is getting a little hard, use a little more pressure.

4 | Using medium-grit sandpaper, lightly sand the surface. This will remove any bumps and also give the façade a slightly "rough" look.

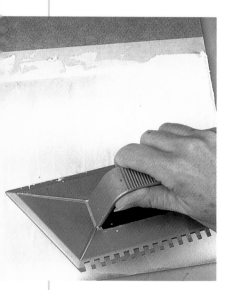

1 | Mix powdered wood putty using three parts water to one part white craft glue to a firm consistency, so that it stands in peaks. Spread it in an even layer about ⅛in thick over an area of wall no larger than you think you can cope with without having to rush.

2 | When the putty is partly dry and no longer sticky (the time this takes varies according to the conditions), score horizontal lines into the wall using a pointed tool and a ruler as a guide. Make these lines a depth of ¹⁄₁₆ to ⅛in and about ¼in apart. Brush off any excess putty.

5 | Test your chosen color on a piece of scrap (a patch of putty spread on cardboard, for example). When you are happy with the effect, paint the wall lightly. You can always add a little more if you want a darker result, but you cannot lighten the color after painting. Another method of application is to dab on the paint using a tight ball of cloth or other coarse material.

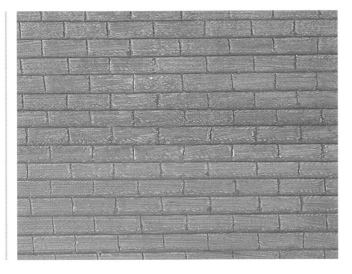

6 | With the base coat complete, you can add "age" to the brickwork by adding further coats of slightly darker colors and shading.

The swatches shown here offer alternative ways to finish the outside walls on the house. Most of these examples use printed paper, but dried foodstuffs and putty have also been used to create texture.

❶ This method is called random stone. Filler is applied to the wall and marked out quite randomly using a pointed marking tool or cocktail stick. Colors of finish may vary depending on the type of stone you are imitating.

❷ Flint walls are sometimes seen in rural locations, where the stone is widely available. This sample is made of split peas adhered to the surface using plenty of white craft glue. When dry the wall is painted in shades of gray.

❸ This example of brickwork printed on paper shows a weathered red brick suitable for the exterior of a Georgian or Victorian house.

❹ Slightly embossed brick effect paper would be ideal for a modern house. The mortar joints are much straighter than in the weathered example. When applying embossed paper, be careful to use minimum pressure to avoid crushing the pattern.

❺ This printed paper is a random stone version. It could be used for an old farmhouse or country cottage. Stone has been used for centuries and fits almost any period.

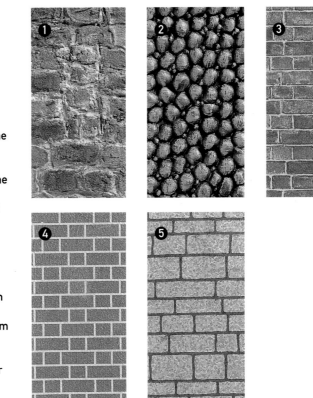

Clapboard siding

CLAPBOARD SIDING, ALSO KNOWN AS FEATHER-EDGE OR WEATHERBOARDING, IS COMMONLY USED IN COUNTRIES WHERE WOOD FOR BUILDING IS WIDELY AVAILABLE. THERE IS NO STANDARD WOOD FOR THIS TYPE OF FAÇADE, WHICH RELIES ON THE AVAILABLE WOOD FROM INDIGENOUS TREES.

The technique is used on wood-frame houses, with the walls usually wood on the outside and made from lathe and plaster internally. There is no standard size for the boards used, but generally in places where severe weather is more common, thicker, heavier boards are used.

Making your own clapboards is not feasible unless you have specialized woodworking equipment. The boards taper from one edge to the other and to do this by hand is not easy. It is recommended that you purchase readymade clapboarding from your dollhouse supplier. You should also consider whether the style of your house is suitable for this type of finish. Townhouses or country mansions, for example, would not look correct with a clapboard façade. A little research will help you to decide if your dollhouse is, in fact, suitable.

☞
Varnishing, page 60

MAKING CLAPBOARD SIDING

Clapboard siding is a simple technique requiring only basic woodwork skills and standard tools. The boarding can be a little expensive, however, if you have a large house to cover. A part-boarded house is an option that can cut costs. This is not an uncommon finish; many real houses are boarded on the upper level with brickwork or painted walls at the ground level. The sheets are normally 2ft long and 3½in wide, so be sure to calculate the amount you need before you buy to avoid purchasing too much.

YOU WILL NEED
For clapboard siding
Sheets of clapboard
Pencil
Razor or tenon saw
Sandpaper
Utility knife
Metal rule
White craft glue
Masking tape
Paint or wood stain
Paintbrushes
Paper towel or cloth
Flat varnish (optional)

1 | Measure the length of board required and mark on the reverse side. Cut to length using a razor or tenon saw. Take care not to cut the piece too small; you can always sand off the ends after the piece has been glued into place. Cut slowly to prevent the edges from fraying. At each cut end, sand lightly with medium-grit sandpaper to remove any burls.

2 | If you need to cut the boarding lengthwise, use a utility knife and a metal rule to guide you. The clapboard is quite thin and should cut easily, avoiding any burls where two sheets need to meet. Any openings for windows or doors should also be cut this way.

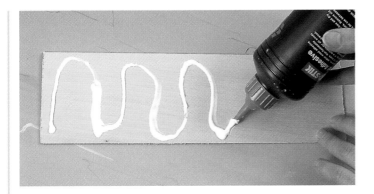

3 | Apply a little white craft glue in lines on the reverse side of the board. There is no need for heavy gluing as the sheets are very light. Place the board on the walls and apply a little pressure. Make sure that any window or door openings are aligned properly.

6 | If you want to add a little extra interest, after the first coat of stain is dry you can paint on knots. Apply dots of a much darker stain onto the walls with a pointed stick.

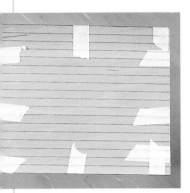

5 | To finish the board, you can paint or stain. Whichever you choose, test first on scraps to get the color right. If you are using stain, use a pale color so that the beauty of the wood shows through. Use solvent-based stain as it will not cause the sheets to buckle.

4 | To prevent the board from lifting at the edges, secure with masking tape until the glue has set. Where masking tape is not practical, use thumbtacks to secure. Don't worry about leaving holes; they will look like knots when decorated.

7 | To blend the knots in, brush each one out as you go using a dry brush. Clean the brush on a piece of dry paper towels or cloth. If you want a smudge-resistant finish, you can apply a final coat of flat varnish (see Varnishing, p.60).

Pebbledashing or stucco

PEBBLEDASHING, OR STUCCO, IS USED ON THE EXTERIOR WALLS OF HOUSES BOTH AS A DECORATIVE FINISH AND TO PROTECT WALLS FROM THE WEATHER. IT LOOKS PARTICULARLY ATTRACTIVE ON COTTAGES, FARMHOUSES, AND BEACH HOUSES.

Pebbledashing the exterior walls of houses probably sprang from the art of pebble mosaic, which dates back to the 7th century B.C. It is still used today both as a decorative finish, but more important, it protects the walls and in particular the mortar from attack from the ravages of the weather. This type of finish to your dollhouse can look very pleasing, particularly if you are decorating a European-style cottage, farmhouse, village store, or beach house. The materials we use might surprise you, but after many trials and years of practice, it was discovered that dried grains, seeds, etc. work very well. A visit to a health food store will give you some idea of the variety available. Seeds come in a huge choice of sizes and colors, but take care not to choose any that may look too large; $\frac{1}{12}$in should be the absolute maximum diameter, but half that size would be better. The technique is simple and involves applying glue to the exterior wall, then quickly sprinkling seeds on top and pressing down in place.

TIPS OF THE TRADE
When applying "pebbles," always work on an old sheet or blanket, as large as your space allows. Pebbles can get everywhere if you aren't careful. When finished, wrap up your sheet and shake it outside.

PEBBLEDASHING A WALL
Pebbledashing is easy and inexpensive. Before you start to apply the glue, make a pencil mark around all the windows and doors and then take them out. Protect all the areas not to be covered with masking tape, including any moldings. When you apply the glue, try to cover one whole side of the house at once, as jointing can be tricky and messy. Using a large brush, you can paint on the glue in a few minutes.

YOU WILL NEED
To pebbledash a wall
Seeds and grains
White craft glue
2in brush
Masking tape
Small wooden block
Pencil
Spoon

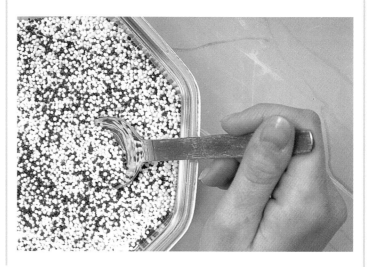

1 Mix a selection of seeds and grains together in a bowl or basin, making sure to get an even blend of color and size. This is most important as it will be too late to change the mixture once it has been applied.

2 | Apply craft glue to the walls using a flat paint brush. Apply glue liberally but not too thickly.

5 | Use the flat side of the piece of wood to press the pebbles gently to make sure they sink into the glue and are stuck fast. Do not use too much pressure.

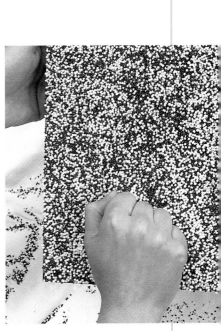

3 | Working with the wall placed horizontally, sprinkle on the "pebbles" evenly with a spoon to a depth of about ¼in. The depth is not critical, but make sure that the whole surface is evenly covered and no holes are left.

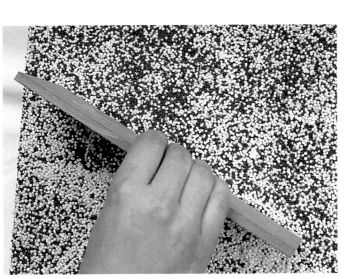

4 | Rake over the pebbled area with a straight-edged piece of wood to even out the pebbles and remove excess material.

6 | Leave to set overnight in a dry place. To remove pebbles that are not securely stuck, stand the house upright and rap the surface smartly. Do this a few times until no more pebbles fall off. Repeat the operation on all sides of the house.

Pillaring

PILLARS HAVE BEEN USED IN
BUILDINGS SINCE THE BEGINNING
OF ARCHITECTURE. IF THE DESIGN OF
YOUR DOLLHOUSE ALLOWS THEIR
USE, THEY CREATE A GREAT
IMPRESSION.

The use of pillars as structural supports is as old as building itself. Pillars are of course much more than this and for centuries have been an important part of the design as well as the construction of building, from the modest townhouse to the grandeur of such buildings as the White House in Washington, the Bank of England in London, and countless other fine examples around the world. Even a small portico or porch on the façade of any house will add a great deal.

The making of pillars is simplicity itself; if you can cut a piece of wood straight, you can make your own; and if you have a miter block, you can cut any piece of wood straight, as long as it fits into your block.

CHOOSING MATERIALS For your pillars you will need a length of round wood approximately 1in in diameter. You may, of course, choose any thickness that suits your design or you may even choose a square section if you prefer. Doweling is the obvious choice as it comes in all sizes and is not too expensive, but you may have an old broom or mop handle that you can use instead.

Decide whether you want the pillars to go straight from floor to ceiling or to stand on a plinth. Plinths are simple to make; you need to cut flat wood about ½in thick into squares of different sizes ranging from 1½in upward, depending on how high you want the plinth to be. Carefully measure the length required, allowing for any base you are going to stand the pillar on. Using your miter block, cut the wood square

Faux marbling, page 46

with a razor saw, checking each length you cut to make certain they are all the same. If you do decide to use a plinth, glue the pieces together with fast white craft glue before putting them in place. When you have all your components cut, it is far easier to decorate them on your workbench than in situ. However, plinths should be mounted on the pillars before decoration. Generally, pillars are painted in the same color and paint as the main building, but in some cases marble pillars are used (see page 46).

TIPS OF THE TRADE
Always mark the position of all the pillars on the floor before you begin to glue. This is important as they cannot be moved afterward.

PILLARING
The use of pillars is a simple way to create an eye-catching "grand" effect. Plan carefully how many pillars you will need and where you will place them. An English-style townhouse may use pillars to support a small roof over the front door; a grand mansion in Virginia may use them in profusion along the length of the façade. The following method can be used to make pillars whatever effect you aim to create.

YOU WILL NEED
For pillaring
Wood
Miter block
Rule/measure and pencil
Razor saw
Sandpaper
White craft fast glue
Paint
Brushes

1 | Choose a length of round wood of the diameter you require. Place the uncut wood against the roof to be supported. Stand it on the plinth, if you are using one. Carefully mark the height to the underside of the roof using a sharp pencil. A blunt end gives a thick line and is less accurate.

2 | Place the wood in the miter block and cut along the marked line carefully using a razor saw. Be sure to keep the work piece steady as you saw and do not rush as this may result in badly fitting ends.

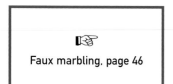

3 | Check the position of the pillar and plinth. When you are satisfied with the placement of the plinth on the floor and the pillar on the plinth, mark their positions with a sharp pencil. Remove and put to one side for decorating. This should be done before final gluing.

4 | When the pillars and plinth (if used) are decorated, carefully glue the pillar to the plinth using fast white craft glue or wood glue. When it is dry, apply glue to the top of the pillar and the bottom of the plinth and place it in the previously marked position.

MAKING A PLINTH FOR A PILLAR

The plinths for pillars may be square, made in two or more pieces, or they may be round, or a combination of both. Whatever design you choose, it is important to cut them accurately. Badly cut plinths can ruin the effect. If you do make a mistake, discard the plinth and cut another. Material costs are minimal.

YOU WILL NEED
For a plinth
Piece of wood
Pencil
Razor or tenon saw
Vise
Sandpaper
Wood glue
"C" clamp

1 | Stand the pillar on a piece of wood or board of the chosen thickness and mark the size of the upper section of the plinth you require. Allow about ½in from the pillar to the edge of the plinth. Normally for a two-piece plinth, the larger base section is about ½in larger than the upper section all around.

2 | When satisfied that the marking is correct, cut carefully using a razor or tenon saw. Take your time and cut accurately. It may help to steady the workpiece in a vise if you have one. Clean off rough edges with medium-grit sandpaper, and finally with fine sandpaper to give a smooth finish.

3 | When you have finished the upper section, place it on the wood again and mark the base section about ½in larger all around. These measurements can, of course, be altered if they do not suit your requirements. Cut and finish as before. When both of the pieces are made to your satisfaction, glue them together using quick-drying wood glue.

Quoining

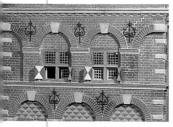

QUOIN STONES ARE SET AT THE EXTERNAL ANGLE OR CORNER OF A HOUSE. THEY ACT AS STRUCTURAL SUPPORTS AND AS DECORATIVE FEATURES TO CONTRAST WITH THE BRICKWORK OR MASONRY OF THE MAIN WALLS.

Quoining dates back to ancient Rome and has been in use in western architecture down the ages. It can be found on a variety of buildings, from humble 18th-century French cottages where the stones were heavily rusticated, to the Vatican in Rome, Buckingham Palace in London, and Mount Pleasant in Philadelphia. Quoins are also used around other openings, such as windows and doors, albeit in grander architecture. They were used extensively in the building of large houses around the world in the English Renaissance style.

Making your own stones is quite time-consuming, since all the edges have to be chamfered. No special skill is needed, but a good eye and steady hand will make your job easier. You can, of course, purchase stones from your local supplier, but they tend to be expensive and the choice of sizes is not generally great. If your house is to be "of an age," handmade quoins look much better as they should not be quite perfect.

Quoins can be made from thin strips of particle board or heavy cardboard. There is no standard size, but, as a guide, they are usually set in two sizes, one being twice the length of the other: 1in × 1½in and 1in × ¾in. To make your own quoins, you need strips of plywood or cardboard 1in wide; the length will depend upon how many you need to make. Plywood is recommended for quoining as it is more durable, it is easier to chamfer the edges, and it takes paint better.

Measure the height of your dollhouse corners in inches; the total number of inches tells you how many

Textured external paint finishes, page 92

stones you will need. Bear in mind that half of the stones will be 1½in long and half will be 1in long. Cut your stones using a fine-toothed razor saw and a small miter block.

It is recommended that you paint the stones on your workbench, as it is very difficult not to get paint on your main walls if they are positioned first. You should also have finished the main decoration to the outside of your house before positioning the quoins. Mark the edge where you are placing the quoins to keep paint off. To position the quoins, start at the bottom of your walls with one large stone, then add one small stone to make a toothed effect, and work up until you reach the top. If your top stone is less than ½in wide it would be best to leave this off as it can look a little odd if it is too small. To fix your stones, first make sure no paint is left on the reverse side as it may stop them laying flat. A light sanding of the surface is recommended. Glue each stone in place using a fast white craft wood glue.

PLACING QUOIN STONES
First determine how many quoin stones you need and the size you want them to be. Generally, a large house will need larger stones than a smaller one. Whether you choose cardboard or particle board for your stones depends upon the finish you want and the amount of time you have. Particleboard stones take longer to make since the edges have to be chamfered. Cardboard stones are simple to make, requiring no more than a pair of good scissors. Here, particleboard has been used.

YOU WILL NEED
Placing quoin stones
Saw
Particleboard
File
Paint
Brush
White craft glue
Miter block
Sandpaper
Masking tape

1 | Have lengths of particleboard cut at your local lumber yard or craft store. Using the miter block, cut the "stones" to required length, remembering that you need two different sizes. For this house the stores were 1 x 1½in and 1 x ¾in.

2 Using a file, chamfer all four edges; only slightly file so that when the stones are butted together they form a "v" shape at the join.

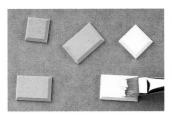

3 Sand each stone with medium-grit sandpaper. Decide what color will look best with the main walls and paint the stones with latex paint using a flat brush. When thoroughly dry, check that no bubbles have appeared. If this is the case, sand with extra fine sandpaper.

4 Starting at the bottom of the wall, glue a large stone in place. Alternate large and small stones. Use masking tape to hold each stone in place until the glue has dried.

ANTIQUING EXTERIOR QUOIN STONES

Antiquing quoin stones makes exterior stonework look weathered and therefore looks consistent with an antiqued façade (see Textured exterior paint finishes, page 92). Before you start antiquing, the stones (whether purchased or homemade) must be painted with an off-white undercoat. This can be made by adding a little raw sienna acrylic paint to a white base color. You can also buy premixed small sample jars of paint from hardware stores. When the first coat of undercoat is dry, stick the quoin stones to the façade with some white craft glue. You are now ready to start antiquing.

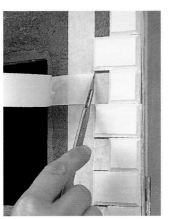

1 Make sure all exterior paintwork is dry. Then mask out the areas around the quoin stones using 1in masking tape. This will prevent any paint from dripping onto the prepainted façade.

YOU WILL NEED
For antiquing
Masking tape
Acrylic paint
Acrylic matt medium
Lint-free cloth
½in brush
Glaze
Sponge

2 Mix a transparent glaze by adding a little raw umber acrylic paint to acrylic matt medium.

3 Wrap a lint-free cloth around your finger. Dip it into the glaze and gently rub it into the quoin stones. Work across the stones, making sure that the grooves and edges are covered.

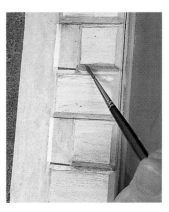

4 With a ½in brush, paint glaze into the grooves between the stones. This will enhance the three-dimensional effect. The lighter flat areas will come forward while the darker grooves will recede. Apply the paint in thin layers, trying not to create lumps or drips.

5 Finally, further reinforce the impression of depth by adding highlights with a white glaze applied with a natural sponge. Drag the glaze across the surface of the stones. If you wish, you can add a lichen effect as described on page 94.

Textured external paint finishes

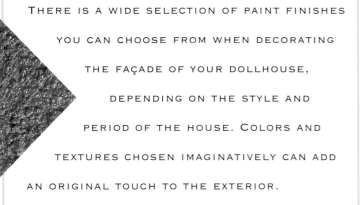

THERE IS A WIDE SELECTION OF PAINT FINISHES YOU CAN CHOOSE FROM WHEN DECORATING THE FAÇADE OF YOUR DOLLHOUSE, DEPENDING ON THE STYLE AND PERIOD OF THE HOUSE. COLORS AND TEXTURES CHOSEN IMAGINATIVELY CAN ADD AN ORIGINAL TOUCH TO THE EXTERIOR.

The most arresting feature of a dollhouse is its façade, and you can make a strong impression with color and texture. Historically, many colors have been used to decorate exteriors, ranging from an olive green townhouse to a pink cottage.

There is a wide choice of paint products and mediums available to create different paint finishes. First, start with a color combination you like, then think about texture. It is always a good idea to mix up a few colors and test various combinations before you make your final choice. Home-decorating stores should have color swatch charts you can refer to, along with small sample jars of paint.

Once you have decided on colors, then think about texture. Masonry paints are ideal for creating texture on an exterior of a cottage or farmhouse, as they imitate the gritty finish of sandstone. They are available in authentic external color schemes, and they are quick drying and easy to apply.

SPATTERING Spattering simulates the look of lichen or moss, which is a natural fungus that forms on the front of buildings and stone work. A hand-rendered effect using paint can look very effective on a dollhouse façade and on decorative corbels. After glazing the façade, apply the spattering while the glaze is still wet, using a toothbrush or a coarse dry paintbrush. Spatter a mixture of raw sienna and sap green paint with a bit of yellow ocher to add brightness over the glaze. This will create a subtle speckling

upon the glazed surface. Finally, seal the surface with a flat water-based varnish.

SPONGING Sponging creates a subtle, softly textured effect on paintwork. The softness and quality of marking depends on the type of sponge used; for a dollhouse, a suitable choice would be a small natural sponge. You can sponge exterior walls and decorative corbels to create a mottled finish to simulate the effects of aging. Always work wet into wet when sponging as this helps the colors to merge, and try to stick to a simple color scheme. Experiment with a few samples to test the possibilities before you start to paint. This technique is very effective when worked into wet glaze on the outside of a building.

☞

Preparing the surface,
page 16
Handpainted walls, page 38

ADDING TEXTURE

This handpainted technique is used to create a textured finish on external walls, adding age and character to the frontage. This rustic look is suitable for a country cottage or farmhouse. Before applying the textured filler, decide whether you are going to add quoin stones or any other type of decorative feature to the external walls.

YOU WILL NEED

For handpainting
Thin cardboard
Putty
Sponge
Sandpaper
Acrylic varnish
Acrylic glaze
Acrylic paints: burnt
    umber, ultramarine, raw
    sienna
Masonry paints
2 × 2in brushes
Soft 2in or 3in brush
Paper towels
Soft rag

1 The first stage is to add texture to the outer walls. Use putty mixed to a thick creamy paste (one part water to two parts filler). Apply the putty to the walls using a thin piece of cardboard to form a layer approximately ⅛in thick.

5 | Using the corner of the cardboard, remove a border about ⅜in wide from around the outside of the window to create a flat outer channel for the window frame.

2 | When applying the putty, drag the cardboard across the wall horizontally, creating a one-directional effect. Work quickly to achieve the desired thickness before the putty dries. It is usually best to work in sections.

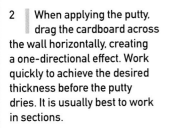

4 | Once the texture has been applied, remove any excess from around the windows, making sure there is no putty on the inside of the frame. If the putty dries around the windows, it will be difficult to glue in the window frames. You may have to rub lightly with fine sandpaper to achieve a smooth surface.

3 | Add the surface texture while the putty is still moist. Using a fine-textured sponge, press lightly into the putty. Work quickly across the whole area in this way.

6 | If you are going to apply quoin stones (see page 90) to the corners, you will need to remove the putty from these areas, too.

7 | Masonary paint is best for textured exterior work. Apply the desired color with a sponge to further emphasize the texture. There is no need to thin the paint.

9 | Blot any excess glaze with a natural sponge, rubbing back to the ground color in selected areas to create an uneven surface. Remove any excess paint with paper towels.

10 | Pat dry with a soft rag or sponge. When dry, lightly sand with a fine abrasive to create a subtle distressed effect.

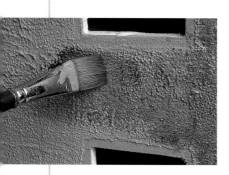

8 | When the base color is dry, lay the house on its back with the front facing upward. Mix a thin acrylic glaze to a watery consistency, adding a small amount of acrylic matt or gloss medium to the desired color. If you want an old, weathered effect, use earth colors such as raw umber or burnt umber. Raw umber has a dull finish, while burnt umber is more translucent. If you want to make the glaze warmer, add a touch of burnt sienna or raw sienna. Mix the colors with some matt or satin medium and apply with a brush. Apply the glaze in even brushstrokes. Be careful not to let the paint run.

11 | After sanding you may want to add another layer of glaze in a richer color. Here a thin wash of ultramarine was mixed with raw sienna, but other earth colors would be equally effective.

SPATTERING TECHNIQUE FOR LICHEN EFFECT

Spattering simulates the look of lichen or moss, which is a natural algal fungus that forms on the front of buildings and stonework. A hand-rendered effect using paint can look very effective on your dollhouse facade and decorative corbels. After glazing the façade, apply the spattering while it is still wet, using a toothbrush or a dry coarse paintbrush. Spatter a mixture of raw sienna and sap green or a bit of yellow ocher to add brightness. This creates a subtle speckling on the glazed surface. The final stage is to seal with a flat water-based varnish.

The same principle can be applied to architectural details and stonework, which may benefit from this weathering process. On an old building, the effect of moss or lichen can be worked into the façade.

YOU WILL NEED

Spattering
Sap green paint
Raw sienna or yellow ocher paint
Toothbrush or coarse dry paintbrush
Wet glaze
Acrylic matt medium

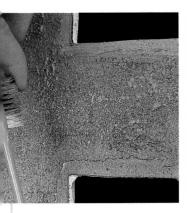

Mix yellow ocher and sap green into a fluid glaze. As acrylic dries fast, you may need to work with some speed. Experiment on a piece of cardboard painted in the same color as your house before you start. Use an old toothbrush. Fill the brush with paint. Slowly pull your fingers over the ends, allowing the paint to spray onto the surface. Once the paint is dry, apply another spattering of color to add to the richness and depth of the effect.

SPONGING

Sponging creates subtle, soft effects on paintwork. The softness and quality of marking depends on the type of sponge used. For a dollhouse a small natural sponge is the best choice. You can apply this technique to exterior walls and decorative corbels to create a mottled finish that can simulate the effects of aging.

Always work wet into wet when sponging as this helps the colors to merge. Try to keep to a limited range of colors. Test the possibilities with a few trial samples. This technique is particularly effective when worked into a wet glaze on the outside of a dollhouse.

YOU WILL NEED
Sponging
Natural sponge
Acrylic paints
Acrylic varnish
Paper

Work into the wet green dabbing with the natural sponge. Once the paint is dry, dab on color to add to richness and depth.

The paint finish you give to the exterior of your dollhouse sets the tone for the style of interiors within. The techniques illustrated here show a variety of exteriors appropriate for modern and period townhouses and country cottages.

❶ A traditional color for country cottages in the eastern counties of England, this gritty textured paint could be painted directly onto a dollhouse façade or onto a rough rendered finish.

❷ This textured stone finish is achieved by sponging acrylic texture gel onto particleboard. When dry paint with a mix of white, raw umber, and raw sienna to create a granite-like effect.

❸ The impression of rough stonework can be created by applying filler to the walls and scoring into it before it dries. Paint with a mix of white, raw umber, and burnt umber. This finish would be ideal for a farmhouse and could be used in conjunction with red brick quoining.

❹ Walls with this type of rendered finish usually have brickwork around the windows and doors. Apply a mixture of sand, red oxide paint, and acrylic texture gel directly to the walls.

❺ Rough plaster is traditionally applied to a wooden façade for added durability. The effect shown here was achieved by applying acrylic texture gel to the dollhouse walls. When dry it was painted white.

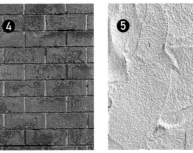

Trellising

SMALL PANELS OF TRELLIS CAN WORK WELL PLACED ON EACH SIDE OF THE FRONT DOOR OF A DOLLHOUSE, FRAMING IT VISUALLY. A BURST OF COLOR CAN BE ADDED BY BUILDING UP A SIMPLE IMPRESSION OF FOLIAGE, CLIMBING PLANTS, AND FLOWERS GROWING THROUGH THE TRELLIS.

Trellising is a technique applied to the exterior of a house. It is in fact the copying in miniature of the panels of a garden trellis which adorn the front of a house or cottage and is suitable for many dollhouses. For inspiration, look at gardening books or home decorating magazines which will show you how trelliswork can be arranged. You may need some reference on plants and flowers to give you ideas of how to create floral effects over the framework. The technique is not an exact science; you will need to improvise, perhaps using colored papers and the many scenic materials available. You may also want to incorporate real foliage in your trellising. Before you do, check that the scale is in keeping with the rest of the house.

YOU WILL NEED
To make trellis
Wooden slats ⅛in square
Metal square
Wood glue
Saw
Cocktail stick or sharpened match
Utility knife
Sandpaper
Brush
Wood stain

MAKING A TRELLIS
Make sure that the bars are not too thick, as they can look out of scale. For most dollhouses, wooden slats about ⅛in square are the correct size. You will need a workboard with at least one good straightedge to set your square against. Make the outside frame of the trellis as square as you can. The inside slats can be slightly less accurate as these will be concealed by the "plants."

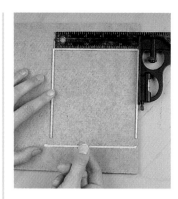

1 | Decide on the size of your finished panel of trellis. Cut two horizontal and two vertical lengths to make a frame for your trellis. Cut carefully using the square to make sure the slats are a consistent length. Bad fitting may cause the whole structure to collapse. Glue the pieces together with a dab of quick-drying wood glue to form a rectangular frame.

2 | When your outside square is set, cut the cross pieces carefully. Be sure after each cut that every length fits perfectly. Spread a little glue on some scrap wood, not too thickly. Dab the ends of the cross pieces into this one at a time and reposition on the frame. Don't pick up too much glue as this can make a mess.

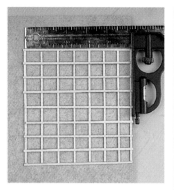

3 | After this section is set, turn the trellis over. Cut the uprights as before, checking each as you go. Glue each end and, in addition, using a cocktail stick or sharpened match, dab a little glue at the intersection with the cross pieces before you position them.

4 | When the whole trellis is set, remove any excess glue left on the surface with a utility knife or medium-grit sandpaper. Stain the trellis the color of your choice. Green or brown are popular for gardens. Try a little on a scrap before you paint the trellis itself.

DRESSING A TRELLIS

What could be nicer around your front door than a display of flowers or foliage? The choice is unlimited. Many craft stores and modelmaking suppliers carry a large selection of suitable products, or you can visit your local florist, where they probably stock miniature dried flowers and foliage.

YOU WILL NEED
Dressing trellis
Foliage
Multipurpose glue
Oil-based paint
½in brush
Utility knife or scissors
Trelliswork

2 | The ferns are soft and pliable, and can be bent and shaped as required. When you have determined how you want to position the fern, dab a little multipurpose glue on the reverse side of each fern and stick it to the trellis.

4 | Add other colors to the foliage, depending upon the effect you want to achieve. Use a small brush and dab the paint rather than brushing.

6 | Weave the foliage in a vine-like fashion through the trellis, with the majority of leaves on the outward side. Flatten any leaves on the inside, so that the trellis will lie flat against the wall. There is no need for glue as the leaves will hook behind the slats and hold themselves in place.

1 | The miniature ferns (left) and miniature branches with leaves (right) are examples of the types of products available from craft stores. The latter are stamped out of a thin brass sheet. It is a good idea to visit a few places before you make your final choice.

3 | Paint brass leaves green using oil-based paint. Water-based paint will not adhere well. Be sure to paint the edges of the leaves, because when you bend them into shape later they will be exposed.

5 | When the paint is dry, cut out the branches and leaves using a utility knife or a pair of scissors. Bend and twist the leaves and stems until you have a natural-looking three-dimensional effect. The branches can be as long or short as you wish.

7 | You are now ready to glue the trellis in place on the wall. Make sure that all the external decoration of the façade is complete. Dab spots of multipurpose glue on the back of the trellis and press it in place. If you think you may wish to change the dressing in the future, the trellis can be "hung" on pins for easy removal. These can be hidden behind foliage.

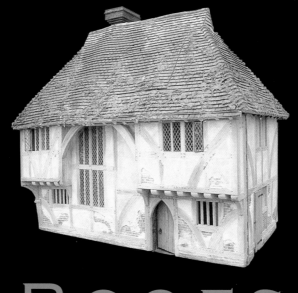

ROOFS

Simple roofing

THE ROOF OF ANY BUILDING IS AN IMPORTANT PART OF THE CONSTRUCTION, SERVING AS A BARRIER TO PROTECT AGAINST THE WEATHER. IN DOLLHOUSE CONSTRUCTION, A DOUBLE SLOPE OR GABLED ROOF IS THE MOST COMMONLY USED, AND THE COVERING IS GENERALLY THE EFFECT OF SLATE, CLAY TILES, OR INTERLOCKING SHINGLES.

Down through the ages, many forms of roofs were built in a wide variety of forms, including flat, single pitch, double pitch, vaulted, domed, or sometimes in a combination as dictated by technical, economic, or esthetic considerations. A double slope or gabled roof is most commonly used for dollhouses, and the covering is either slate, clay tiles or more recently interlocking shingles.

DRAWN TILES A good and simple way to achieve the effect of slate roofing is to draw the slates using a pencil. This method is inexpensive and simple. If you have a little gray paint (or other color, if you prefer) and some leftover varnish, then you can slate your roof for free! Careful measurement and a steady hand is all you need.

DRAWN TILES

Drawing tiles directly onto the dollhouse roof is one of the simplest ways of achieving a roof.

1 | Paint the roof with your chosen color then set out the measurements. The finished slates are 1in square, so mark 1in divisions up both sides of the roof, starting at the bottom. With a pencil and straightedge, draw horizontal lines across the roof until complete.

YOU WILL NEED

For simple roofing
Paint
Brush
Pencil
Straightedge
Flat varnish

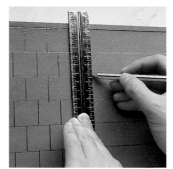

2 | Mark the center of the roof on the bottom edge. From this starting point, measure 1in divisions sideways in each direction. Draw vertical lines to join the first and second horizontal lines. On the next course, mark the vertical lines halfway along each slate on the course below to create a staggered effect. Continue until you have drawn all the slates. If you make a mistake, you can correct it by erasing the lines and re-drawing.

3 | When all the lines are drawn and you feel happy with the result, brush the roof to remove any pencil dust. To seal the roof and give it an old appearance, finish with a coat of flat varnish.

Slate and tile roofs

ON THE FOLLOWING PAGES WE WILL SHOW YOU HOW TO ACHIEVE DIFFERENT ROOFING EFFECTS. SOME ARE MORE TIME-CONSUMING THAN OTHERS. BUT NONE IS BEYOND YOU IF YOU POSSESS BASIC WOODCRAFT SKILLS.

Generally, the roof is the first part of the house to be finished, as you do not want any dust or paint falling on other finished work. Making the basic slate or shingle requires thin strips of plywood or cardboard, but, for durability, ¹⁄₁₆in-thick plywood is recommended, birch-faced if possible. In the U.S., slate comes mainly from Pennsylvania and Vermont, and in Europe Welsh slate is widely used. Slate comes in many colors, but for roofing, gray is most common. Clay tiles are also found worldwide and in many colors.

No special tools or materials are needed for roofing. For ridge tiles, in all cases use 1in angle beading, sometimes called "cushion cover," cut into 1¹⁄₂in strips and butted together end to end. Paint should always be a flat finish undercoat, or flat latex. If you choose to use cardboard instead of plywood, when you are gluing, use a solvent-based glue, as water-based glue may cause cardboard to separate or buckle.

SLATE ROOFS The type of roof on your dollhouse will, of course, depend upon the style, period, and geographical location. One of the most common types of roofing for dollhouses is slate. There are several ways of achieving a slate finish, from a painted effect to "slates" made from thin plywood, or you can actually buy real miniature slates made by hand to scale.

☞
Varnishing, page 60

MAKING PLYWOOD SLATES

Making your own slates from thin plywood is quite simple, requiring only basic woodworking skills. As with most tasks, good tools and sharp blades and saws will make your job much easier. There are two methods to choose from. The first is to make individual slates using strips of ¹⁄₁₆in plywood, cut into lengths 1¹⁄₂in wide and then cut off in 1in pieces. Alternatively, you can keep the lengths in one piece and cut slots 1in apart and 1in from the bottom edge upward. The latter method is shown here.

YOU WILL NEED
For making plywood slates
Thin sheets of plywood
Pencil
Metal rule
Utility knife

TIPS OF THE TRADE
When cutting several pieces of plywood or cardboard, make a "jig" by marking the length from the center line with white masking tape on the miter block.

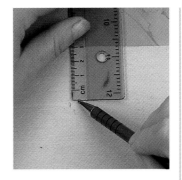

1 | Make marks to a depth of 1¹⁄₂in along one edge of a sheet of ¹⁄₁₆in plywood. The length of the strip should be slightly longer than the length of the roof.

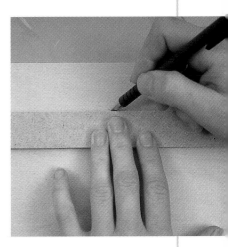

2 | Using a rule, draw a line joining up all the marks.

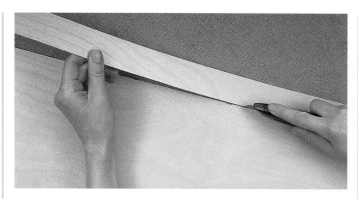

3 | Cut along the line with a utility knife with a new blade. If your hand is steady, cut freehand, which will give the finished row of "slates" a convincing, slightly uneven look. If, however, you want straighter lines, use a metal rule as a guide.

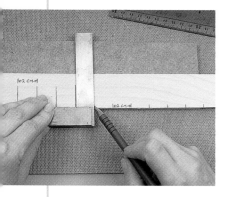

4 | Mark individual tiles to the width you require – about 1in is a usual size. Mark the depth of the tiles – about 1in in this example – with parallel ruled lines. Absolute precision is not required, since slight discrepancies can enhance the look of the finished roof.

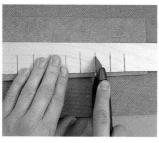

5 | Cut through the pencil lines using a utility knife with a new blade.

6 | To obtain a thicker, more defined line between the slates, use a tenon saw and miter block to cut the divisions. If you want the house to look old, you may decide to use individual slates, so that some may be laid "slipped" to give a dilapidated look. If so, cut the divisions all the way through and you will be left with single slates.

TILING YOUR ROOF WITH HANDMADE SLATES

The method described for making slates by hand using thin plywood also applies to the use of thick cardboard. The cardboard method is cheaper and arguably easier, but not so durable. The main difference is that solvent-based glue must be used, since a water-based white craft glue may cause cardboard to separate and buckle. When using cardboard tiles, do not make good at the gable ends using putty, but cover with a gable-end facia.

1 | Glue a length of wood ⅛in by ⅛in at the eaves flush with the leading edge, using white craft glue or other wood glue. This will lift the first course of slates and allow all subsequent courses to lie flat. Let it dry completely. Don't be tempted to start the next stage too soon; if this piece moves, it can spoil the rest of your hard work. Mark a center line on the roof from top to bottom.

YOU WILL NEED
For tiling with handmade slates
White craft glue
Pencil
Stiff brush
Damp cloth
Masking tape
Utility knife

2 | Cut your strips of "slates" slightly longer than the length of the roof, allowing for the stagger of joints. On the first course, line up the most central joint of the slates with the center line marked on the roof. This should allow you an excess at each end of about ¼in. Trim each end as necessary.

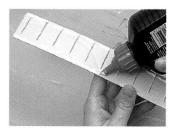

3 | When you are sure that the length of the strip of slates is correct, apply a little glue along both edges. Take care not to use too much glue on the bottom edge, as this may ooze through and fill up the joints.

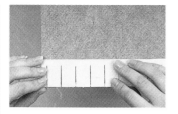

4 Carefully lay the first strip on top of the edging piece so that the slates overlap the edge of the roof by about ⅛in. Remove any excess glue from between the joints before it begins to dry with a stiff brush and from the bottom edge with a damp cloth.

5 It is important to make sure the first course is correctly positioned as it sets the pattern for all subsequent courses. Be sure that the overlap at the bottom edge of the roof is even. Use masking tape at each end and in the center to hold the strip in place. Let the glue dry properly before proceeding.

6 Continue to lay strips up the roof slope, staggering each course as shown. The middle joint of alternate courses should line up with the center mark on the roof. Great precision is not required as real roofs are seldom accurate, but be careful not to allow the degree of error to become excessive. When you reach the ridge, mark the last course and trim off any excess before gluing.

> **TIPS OF THE TRADE**
> If any lengths of slates bulge in the center, use a small piece of masking tape to hold them in place.

RIDGE TILES
The finish of a tiled or slate roof is the ridge. If you are using single tiles for the "older" look, cut 1in angle beading or cushion corner into 1½in lengths and glue them into place butted together. If you are using strips of tiles, use the alternative method shown here, in which one continuous length of wood is used.

1 Measure the length of the ridge by placing the beading along the roof and marking it with a pencil. Cut to length with a tenon or razor saw, allowing ¹⁄₁₆in extra at each end to allow for sanding at the final stage. Mark the ridge tiles 1½in apart. Use a tenon saw to score to a depth of about ¹⁄₁₆in along the pencil lines. Be sure to score the lines all around the ridge. Rub over lightly with coarse sandpaper.

YOU WILL NEED
For ridge tiles
Wood beading
Pencil
Tenon or razor saw
Sandpaper (coarse and medium-grit)
Masking tape
White craft glue
Stiff brush
Damp cloth
Wood putty
Plastic spatula or putty knife

2 Apply a line of white craft glue along both internal edges of the ridge piece but not into the "well" at the bottom. Be sparing with the glue to prevent excess from oozing out from the sides.

3 | Place the ridge piece on the apex of the roof so that it sits squarely. When you are sure that it is correctly positioned, use masking tape to hold down the ends, as they tend to curl up. Wipe away any excess glue with a damp cloth. Excess glue can be removed from the joints with a stiff brush.

4 | When all the glue is thoroughly dry and set, fill the gaps on the gable ends between the tiles and the roof with wood putty applied with a putty knife or plastic spatula. Let it dry thoroughly and sand with medium-grit sandpaper.

PAINTING THE ROOF

The color of the roof of your dollhouse is, of course, a matter of personal choice, but gray slate is widely used. To achieve depth of color, two coats are recommended. The second coat gives a textured appearance to the finished roof.

YOU WILL NEED
For painting
Paintbrush
Oil-based or water-based latex paint
Dry brush
Powdered putty
Nail brush

1 | Choose a base color that is a shade lighter than the top coat, or the end result may be darker than desired. To be sure of your choice, test on scraps. Using a lightly loaded brush, apply paint evenly, pushing the paint into the joints and not forgetting to paint the bottom edge of the slates.

2 | Before the paint begins to dry, remove excess paint from the joints with downward strokes of a dry brush. Run your brush along the bottom edge of the slates to remove any build-up of paint.

3 | When the first coat is dry, spread out a thin layer of paint for the top coat on a board. If you want a textured effect, mix in a little powdered putty. Pick up a little paint with an old nail brush. Too much paint will result in blobs on the roof. Tap off any excess on a clean piece of board.

4 | Carefully apply paint to the roof by dabbing it on lightly. Let a little of the base coat show through, as this gives a realistic depth of color. If any paint is applied too thickly, clean the nail brush and use it to take off the excess.

5 | The finished roof should look as natural as real slates—a little unevenly laid with some slates slipped, and an uneven color. If you notice any large blobs that could not be taken off with your brush, carefully pick them off with the point of a utility knife.

FIBER-BASED CLAY TILES

For centuries clay has been used to make roofing tiles in many countries around the world. The technique shown here uses a fiber-based material to create the effect of a clay tile roof. The sheets are available at most dollhouse suppliers and are simple to apply. The choice of colors available is limited, but you can paint the roof the precise color you want after laying and once the glue is thoroughly dry.

YOU WILL NEED

For fiber-based clay tiles
Sheets of fiber-based clay
  tiles
Pencil
Scissors
Cardboard template
  (optional)
White craft glue
Old brush
Damp cloth

1 The fiber-based clay tile sheets come in various sizes. Take care when handling the sheets, particularly in cold weather, as they are prone to cracking or tearing.

2 Carefully measure the sheet on the roof. Mark the dimensions exactly, allowing no excess, as this material cannot easily be sanded, filled, or filed later. You may find it simpler to make a cardboard template and transfer the dimensions to the tile sheet.

3 When you are confident that the sheet is marked correctly, cut carefully using scissors. If you have to make more than one cut—for example, around a chimney or dormer window—check each one as you go. You can bend the sheet slightly. but take care not to crack or tear it.

4 Try the whole cut sheet on the roof and check that it fits. Squeeze out some white craft glue onto the reverse side of the sheet and spread it evenly using an old brush, taking care that all the edges and corners are coated. Do not use too much glue, which could make the sheet soggy.

5 Wipe the roof with a cloth to make sure it is clean and dust free. Carefully apply the sheet to the roof and slide it into place. Working from the center, smooth out any bubbles or ridges with the palm of your hand. Do not exert pressure as this can flatten the tile effect on wet sheets. Wipe off any glue with a damp cloth.

ROOFING USING REAL SLATES

The ultimate in roofing if your budget will allow is to use genuine handmade slates. These are quite expensive to buy, but not too difficult to apply. They are, of course, a finished product so they require no painting. No special tools are needed other than a good blade in your hacksaw and a sharp marking tool.

YOU WILL NEED
Using real slates
Roofing slates
Wooden strip
White craft glue
Awl
Hacksaw

1 | Real handmade roofing slates made to perfect scale including the correct thickness are difficult and time-consuming to make, hence the high cost.

2 | Glue a piece of wood to the bottom edge of the roof (see Tiling your roof with handmade slates, p.102). Do not proceed to the next step until the glue has set.

3 | Lay a line of fast-drying white craft glue on the piece of wood you have attached to the bottom edge. Dab a little glue on the top edge of a slate and lay it lengthwise on the bottom of the roof, slightly overlapping the edge. Complete the whole course in this way.

4 | When you reach the end you may need to cut the last slate to length. Lay the slate in place and mark a cut using a sharp pointed tool such as an awl, if you have one, but a sharpened nail will do just as well.

5 | Cut the slate using a small hacksaw with a good blade. Use light strokes; too much pressure will shatter the slate.

6 ▌ For the first upright course, apply a line of glue all along the upper edge of the first course and a dab at the top of each slate where it will touch the roof. Lay these side by side and flush with the bottom edge of the slate below. Take care that they do not overlap each other at the edges.

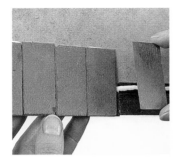

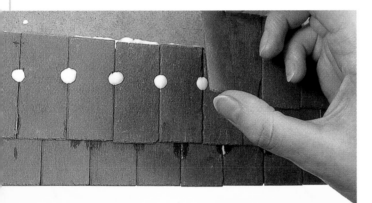

7 ▌ Lay subsequent courses in a similar way, but with each slate staggered halfway across the slate below. Leave 1in of the course below showing. Apply a dab of glue onto each lower slate and to the underside of the slate you are mounting where it touches the roof.

8 ▌ For the ridge, use a course of slates laid sideways and slightly above the top of the roof, so that when you complete the back of the roof, the ridges on both sides will be flush. Use another slate to judge the amount of the overhang.

9 ▌ When finished, your roof should look quite natural with some slates being uneven or "slipped." If, however, you don't want this effect, take a little more care when laying. The bottom edge of each course can be straightened with a ruler before the glue dries.

GALLERY

Wildest dreams

THERE IS NOTHING WRONG WITH SETTING YOUR SIGHTS HIGH. IF YOU DREAM OF CREATING A MINIATURE STATELY HOME, A GRAND TOWNHOUSE, OR AN HISTORIC ROYAL PALACE, WHY NOT PLAN TOWARD THAT GOAL? FOR SUCH PROJECTS, THE STANDARD OF WORK NEEDS TO BE HIGH SINCE THIS IS AN INTRINSIC PART OF THE AMBIENCE. THE MAGNIFICENT STRUCTURES SHOWN WITHIN THIS SECTION WERE ALL BUILT BY PROFESSIONALS. IF BUILDING YOUR OWN HOUSE SEEMS AN IMPOSSIBILITY FOR YOU, YOU CAN BUY A FINISHED BUILDING, A SELF-ASSEMBLY KIT, OR YOU CAN EVEN ORDER YOUR OWN BUILDING FROM A SPECIALIST MAKER. ONCE YOU HAVE THE BASIC STRUCTURE, IT IS THEN POSSIBLE TO DECORATE AND COMPLETE THE FURNISHINGS YOURSELF, THEREBY CREATING YOUR OWN PERSONAL SHOWCASE.

THE PALAZZO VENDRAMIN-CALERGI

The size of your building is obviously a consideration. The model of the Venetian Palazzo Vendramin-Calergi that houses these two rooms is 110in wide, 50in deep, and 86in high. It is virtually impossible to move. In keeping with the grandeur of the building, the finishing techniques employed on its interiors are of the highest standard. The palace, created for a museum, was designed and built by a team led by Peter Mattinson.

▼ Marbled paint effects and wood graining techniques are very much in evidence in the magnificent second-floor grand reception room within this Venetian Renaissance palace. The construction of the model is of wood, but the architectural embellishments are made of a plaster resin mix.

◀ The gentleman's bedchamber, situated on the middle floor of this sumptuous palace, is dominated by a large plaster mantelpiece. Decorative columns, gilded architectural forms, and wall and ceiling finishes have all been completed by hand.

THE CHATEAU DE FONTAINEBLEU

The more magnificent the model, the more splendid the furnishings required to fill it. This elegant French chateau demanded miniature pieces of the very best quality. The work of many of today's top makers is displayed in this superb setting. The chateau, by the construction and design team of Mulvaney and Rogers, was commissioned by Carol and Barry Kaye and is displayed in their Museum of Miniatures in Los Angeles.

▼ As with most replicas of grand buildings being built today, the front façade remains stationary, while the back and sometimes sections of the side panels open to facilitate viewing. Note the weathering and aging techniques that have been used, particularly on the roof, chimneys, and front steps.

▼ Like the rest of the chateau, the Napoleon Library boasts furniture of the highest quality. The marble pillars, arched ceiling form, and painted picture panels provide distinctive period detail.

▶ | The Louis XIII Salon is
perhaps one of the
chateau's finest rooms. It
contains furniture and light
fixtures made by some of the
finest contemporary
craftworkers in the field. There
is also magnificent decorative
detailing, such as the wooden
floor made from individual
pieces and the delicate gilding.

◀ | In the Francis I Gallery, the
detail is staggering.
Special features include the
coffered ceiling, wooden half-
paneled walls, highly polished
floor, and decorative
ornamentation. The chandeliers,
with 12-volt light bulbs, were
specially made.

HAMPTON COURT PALACE

When making a miniature replica of an actual building, whether an historic castle or a copy of your own home, it is usually necessary to make certain adaptations to make it work as a model. For the reproduction of the great Tudor palace of Hampton Court, the design team of Mulvany and Rogers took many, but not all, of the significant features of the original and produced this instantly recognizable result.

▼ In this model of Hampton Court Palace, this is the front façade. The older part of the palace is represented by a section of Anne Boleyn's tower at the side. The top of this is just visible on the right of the picture. Note the weathering and aging effects of both brick and stonework.

▼ This corner of the King's Closet demonstrates the use of a rich color in a miniature setting. A painted marbling effect has been used in the fire surround and hearth. The William and Mary style chair on the left is made from an inexpensive metal kit, skillfully painted to represent wood, cane-work, and fabric.

As the most important ceremonial room in the palace, the Privy Chamber is perhaps the most impressive room in Hampton Court. Seating is intentionally sparse, as only the King would sit during the formal gatherings held within this chamber. Accuracy was the chief concern in creating this room.

▶ This brightly colored little bedchamber from the reign of William III demonstrates how accurate scaling can enhance the overall impact of a decorative scheme. It also contains fine examples of fabric treatments.

AN ARTIST'S HOME

Buildings constructed by professionals need not necessarily be enormous, as this Dutch-style townhouse proves. This small house was commissioned by its owner Cookie Ziemba. The structure of the house together with its internal and external finishes are the work of Peter Mattinson. The interiors were furnished by the owner.

▼ The house was actually based on one in Gorenheim, the Netherlands. However, its owner conceived it as the home of the artist Pieter de Hooch and his family, and set the date of the interiors at around 1660. Judicious aging of the exterior gives this building a strong period feel.

▲ Along with an idea of who might live within a miniature dwelling comes the notion of how it might be furnished. In this example the main parlor of the house would be where the artist and his wife might entertain guests and prospective clients. It is furnished in the manner of the time.

▼ In an upstairs room, all
kinds of domestic tasks
were undertaken, including lace-
making and the spinning of wool.
A cupboard bed, which was
enclosed by curtains at night to
help retain the heat, has been
constructed in the corner.

RENAISSANCE TOWNHOUSE

This model of a merchant's townhouse from northern Germany was created by Cornelia Groh. It is in typical Renaissance style of the late 16th century. Inside the accommodation provided business premises, a family dwelling, and secure storage for merchandise.

▼ The house has been given accurate external architectural detailing with special attention to providing an authentic aged effect. Note the weathered bricks and rust marks from the wall ties.

▲ From the top of the wooden staircase the upstairs hallway leads to the family living quarters and then to a further staircase to the accommodation above. A model's internal layout is perhaps the aspect that is most difficult to achieve.

▼ The large central double doors open onto the spacious main hall with its hard-wearing stone floor. Here trade was carried out, screened from kitchen activities going on behind the windowed wall. The wooden staircase to the left leads to the family accommodation on the upper floors.

DOGE'S PALACE

While such elaborate construction and fine architectural form may be beyond most hobbyist dollhouse makers, this magnificent model of the Doge's Palace in Venice is evidence of what can be achieved by experts. The success of this project is due to the outstanding abilities of its creators, the Modelroom in Kew, near London.

► Some of the carved details were modeled and cast separately, but the paint finishes and aging effects were applied directly to the finished façades. This beautiful window with three-dimensional figures below is part of an end wall of the Doge's Palace.

▲ This project demanded complicated work for the interiors. In the hall of the Ante-Collegio, where ambassadors would await an audience with the Doge, the decoration is highly ornate. The splendid fireplace, elaborate stucco ceiling, and frescoes represent a triumph of miniature achievement.

▶ In the Sala del Collegio, a wide variety of decorative techniques were used in order to recreate the different materials used in the original.

A RANGE OF ROOM SETS

Recreating a miniature room without the restrictions imposed by having to enclose it within the confines of a dollhouse is a project worth considering. The individual room sets shown here take advantage of this freedom and are somewhat larger than might exist within a miniature house.

▼ This period room by Ruth McChesney represents an early 19th-century living room in the area of Chesapeake Bay that might have belonged to a prosperous sea captain. It contains fine furniture and excellent needlework done by the owner herself. Within a room not restricted by external walls, it is possible to give extra dimensions and glimpses of additional spaces beyond.

▲ | Complete with high-quality
▶ | handmade miniatures, the
model of the anteroom of
Spencer House in London was
created. As is apparent from
these two views, she
concentrates on period accuracy
within her historical interiors.

Reflections

IN KEEPING WITH THE CURRENT VOGUE FOR

NOSTALGIA, MOST DOLLHOUSES ARE SET IN A

BYGONE AGE. A HOUSE MAY BE BASED ON A REAL

PLACE, AROUND AN HISTORICAL

CHARACTER, USING AN

ARCHITECTURAL STYLE FROM THE

PAST, OR CONJURED ENTIRELY FROM

THE MAKER'S IMAGINATION. THIS

SECTION INCLUDES MODERN

DOLLHOUSE PROJECTS THAT ARE

SET IN THE PAST. EACH

DEMONSTRATES A DIFFERENCE IN

APPROACH. WHILE THE STYLE OF

THE DOLLHOUSE ITSELF CAN

GOVERN THE PERIOD IN WHICH THE

INTERIORS ARE DECORATED, THIS DOES NOT

ALWAYS NEED TO BE THE CASE. MANY OF US LIVE

IN OLD HOUSES DECORATED IN A MODERN STYLE.

A SCENE SET IN A ROOM BOX OVERCOMES THIS

POSSIBLE DILEMMA.

INSPIRATION FROM OUTSIDE

If the external façade of your dollhouse is strong in character and period style, and its country of origin obvious from its design features, it makes sense to finish the interiors in the same style. This can produce a consistent, coordinated result.

▲ This beautiful townhouse is clearly German in style. It is made from plans and components supplied by Mini Mundus. Here the front opens in two halves, revealing an interior of six rooms. As a bonus, the long roof folds backward, permitting access to an additional three attic rooms. Careful consideration has been given to the front decoration and to the weathered-looking roof tiles.

▲ The interiors are furnished with period pieces and fixtures in total accord with the house. The German-style kitchen, complete with hooded stove, and the arrangement of other rooms are also consistent in style. The placement of figures in the house is a popular idea that helps to enliven the house.

HOUSES FROM HISTORY

These two houses are based on famous real buildings. In each case, their owners have created interiors for them based on careful research and reference to create reproductions that are as faithful as possible to the original.

▼ So keen is the interest in the French Impressionist painter Monet's home at Giverny, that a commercially made dollhouse based upon it is now available. This version has been finished in pink and white with green shutters, in the authentic style of a French country home. Produced in plywood by Honeychurch Toys, England, the house is sold ready for decoration.

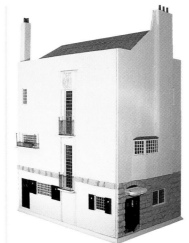

◀ This custom-made artist's townhouse house was commissioned by its owner, who is a great admirer of the work of Charles Rennie Mackintosh. She chose a design Mackintosh was never able to build, even though detailed interior plans were found. The project grew from painstaking research into other Mackintosh buildings, borrowing certain ideas to fill in information that was missing from the designs.

▲ The interior of the artist's house has rooms inspired by various Mackintosh designs. The drawing room decoration and furniture is based on that at South Park in Scotland. The style is instantly recognizable as that of Mackintosh. The house is its owner's tribute to that great designer and artist.

▲ Based on the dining room in Monet's home at Giverny, this brightly colored interior captures the atmosphere of the original. All the materials used, including those for the furniture, were comparatively inexpensive. Pictures of the original were used as reference to guarantee an accurate reproduction of the room.

HOMES FROM THE PAST

A complete family home need not necessarily be that of someone well known or even be completely true to life. One of the houses shown here is a model of a family home. The second is based on a 1775 house in Cambridge, Massachusetts, which although it is still standing, is much changed today. The owner Cookie Ziemba imagined how the house must have been in earlier times and with accurate research created authentic designs.

▶ The furnishings are as Sarah remembers them. Very much in the style of architect Frank Lloyd Wright, the interiors have an atmosphere that reflects that period. The dining room has built-in cabinets complete with opening glazed doors, while light switches are of the old type with black and white on-off push buttons.

◀ This beautifully made house is a 1:12 scale model of a family home in Whittier, California. Built by Pat and Noel Thomas, it was commissioned by collector Sarah Salisbury, whose childhood home it was. The original house was built in the early 1900s by California-based architects. From the tarpaper roof to the glass knobs on the doors, every detail has been accurately reproduced based on either contemporary photographs or on Sarah's own memory.

▼ The music room of the Vassall-Craigie house has the great advantage of side windows through which light can enter and bathe the beautifully decorated room. The furniture is all of excellent quality, and the 48-mesh needlepoint work on the fire screen is by Cookie Ziemba herself.

▲ The exterior of Cookie Ziemba's Vassall-Craigie House is copied from a house in Cambridge, Massachusetts, currently better known as the Longfellow House. Cookie matched the paint color for her model from a chip found on the ground outside when she was visiting the real house.

PERIOD HOUSES WITHOUT HISTORY

Where the structure makes no attempt to copy a well-known character's house or to follow a specific house design, you have the freedom to create a period-style house without being restricted by the need for precise historical accuracy. Within the confines of the broad period you have chosen, you can choose features drawn from many different sources of inspiration.

► This five-story building by Mini Mundus is in the style of a small German townhouse. It offers versatile and flexible accommodation. Here it has been finished as hat and cake shops with living accommodation above. Alternatively, it could have been a department store operating on more than one floor or a hotel. The decorative finish of the exterior should be chosen to give an indication of the accommodation within.

◄ Edwardian houses such as this by Honeychurch Toys, Ltd., sprang up in English suburbs throughout the country. Millions of these houses still exist in Britain, so the interiors could be set at any time from the beginning of the 20th century to the present day.

This house was built for its architectural interest and detail. Based on an existing building in the center of York, England, the model appears as it might have done in the past. Built by Peter Mattinson, it is displayed in The Doll House Museum, Petworth, England.

▲ This Cotswold-style cottage is by The Dollshouse Toys Ltd. The stonework façade has been completed with a paint finish, into which the outline of each stone has been inscribed. The stone roof is made from a flat sheet of cork. This type of cottage could provide the setting for characterful country-style interiors.

REFLECTING A NATIONAL STYLE

Consistency of style is not simply a question of period. Where possible, an interior should reflect the country or region in which it is set. All the interiors shown here are early American, each having its own distinctive period character and style.

▲ In this Federal dining room from about 1785–1815, the repeat pattern wallpaper and the wainscoting are particularly fine. The individual items of furniture are largely based on European designs, but overall this room has an unmistakably American feel. The house is from the Toy and Miniature Museum, Kansas City.

▼ This painted room in a style from around 1750 is the work of Theresa Bahl and other artists. It is from the Toy and Miniature Museum, Kansas City. Of special interest is the delightful hand-painting, the paint-effect marbling of the fire surround, the lack of formality in the arrangement of the room, and the manner in which the walls are divided into panels.

Shaker-style derived from a religious movement of that name that originated in America in the mid-1700s. The religion taught a simple, uncomplicated life, and the homes in which the Shakers lived reflected this ideal. Unnecessary adornment was completely abhorrent to them, and their possessions and furniture were made primarily for their usefulness. Shaker style has had a lasting impact on American design.

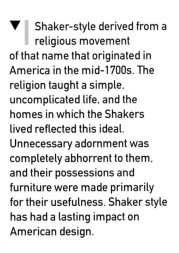

▲ An early settler's home may sometimes have consisted of a single room. Furnishings were made crudely and were of simple design or mimicked forms from the colonists' homeland. Open fireplaces were important for cooking and heating, and bare floorboards and beamed ceilings were typical features.

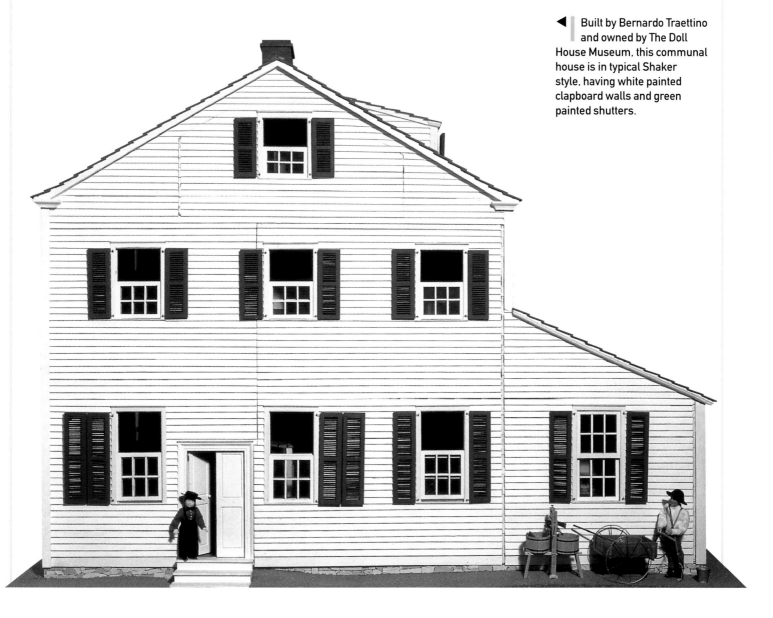

◀ Built by Bernardo Traettino and owned by The Doll House Museum, this communal house is in typical Shaker style, having white painted clapboard walls and green painted shutters.

ACHIEVING HISTORICAL ACCURACY

English interiors of the 15th, 16th, and 17th centuries inspired these three very different rooms. Each was created after extensive historic research by their creators, to whom it was important to get every detail right.

▼ This upper room is in an English style dating from the year 1480. It is based on weavers' houses in the village of Lacock, England. Rooms of this type were designed to accommodate weaving looms. Note the rustic beams, and the impression of wear on the walls and floor. The house with its interiors was built by Peter Mattinson.

▼ This 17th-century room was inspired by the interior of Montacute House, Somerset, England. The Stuart period family who "live" here clearly enjoy music, as the presence of a harpsichord, lute, and early oboe testify.

▲ This 16th century-style dining hall was created by Cookie Ziemba. The wood paneling, fireplace, paintings, and furniture are all accurately detailed to represent those of the era.

SWEDISH STYLE

These three rooms are all based
on Swedish styles from the
18th and 19th centuries. All
three rooms are by Charlotte
Hunt Miniatures, well known
for this type of work.

▼ Based on a palace bedroom
commissioned by Gustav III
of Sweden, who reigned from
1771–91, this room is decorated
and furnished in true Gustavian
style. The walls are white with
gilded paneled moldings, and the
floor is a light polished wood. The
most splendid and perhaps the
most decorative piece in the
room is the tall tiled stove with its
trompe l'oeil decoration.

▲ ⎪ This typical 18th-century
⎪ Gustavian-style dining
room setting employs a
decorative theme of varying
pale grays. This color scheme
was popular at the time and is
the key to the simplicity of the
room. Faux marbling and *trompe
l'oeil* paint effects provide
additional interest.

▶ ⎪ Reminiscent of both Empire
⎪ and Biedermeier styles,
Carl Johan style dates from
1820–50. This British
interpretation uses birch, elm,
and cherry woods in conjunction
with ebony.

VICTORIAN STYLE

The Victorian era is perhaps the most popular style of dollhouse decoration. The period spanned more than 60 years, during which many different styles of interior decoration were used. Nevertheless, most people have an idea of what "Victorian" style means. Each of the three examples shown here represent different interpretations of Victorian style.

▶ From the interior of a pink Painted Lady-style dollhouse, this dining room is instantly recognizable as Victorian. The decorative oil-light chandelier, the red plush upholstered chairs, and the dark wooden door frames and baseboards are all typical of the era.

◀ Built from imagination after considerable research, this hall reflects the taste of West Coast Americans toward the end of the 19th century. The hall has a somewhat informal atmosphere, with its wall covering divided into three patterns.

▲ The decoration of this room from the Guthrie Collection at Hever Castle, Kent, England, is largely Gothic revival. Note the ceiling moldings, mantelpiece, and the mirror. The long button-backed sofa and fireside chairs are perfect choices for Victorian styling.

Remember today

As time rushes by, the present becomes the past all too quickly. One of the charms of antique dollhouses and indeed modern dollhouses set in another age is that they illustrate how lives were led in times gone by. A contemporary miniature setting will all too soon become a record of the past and hold as fascinating a tale for future generations as, say, Victorian life does for us. This final collection of modern rooms provides a record of late 20th-century living, with each taking a slightly different approach.

HOMES FOR MODERN LIFESTYLES

Today there are fewer conformities and conventions to follow than in the past, and perhaps there is therefore greater freedom for us to express our own ideas. Our homes are more varied, too. People make homes in all kinds of buildings, from warehouse lofts to huge homes in the country, and from converted farm buildings to modern high-rise apartment dwellings. With an ever-increasing variety of building and furnishing materials to choose from and more previous design styles to influence us, interiors today are full of imaginative ideas.

▼ This pretty interior by Brooke Tucker Originals might be the envy of any little girl. The miniature dollhouse within the dollhouse provides a lovely finishing touch. Most of the materials and wall coverings are standard dollhouse supplies, but you also need imagination to create a room like this.

▲ The basic plan for this
entrance hall comes from
one of Brooke Tucker's courses.
Each student is encouraged to
create his or her own design for
the decoration of the finished
room. The elegant result
achieved here is the work of
Ray Whitledge.

THE HIGH LIFE

Many modern city-dwellers choose to make their homes in high-rise apartment buildings. In most cases, the rooms are on one level, which can allow living areas to flow easily from one to the other, giving a wonderful impression of space. The recreation of this type of home in miniature can be great fun, and there is the bonus of not needing to take up precious space with a hall and staircase.

▼ Ray Whitledge, the creator of this elegant penthouse suite has imagined that it is located in a suburb of Washington, DC, and has views of the Potomac River and the prominent monuments and buildings beyond. The use of a window with a scene set behind is an inventive way of giving a room set an extra dimension.

▲ Designed by Brooke Tucker Originals to house a collection of miniatures, this set of rooms is full of accessory detail. Note the open arch between one room and the one beyond.

► This bedroom is entitled "San Francisco Splendour." The atmosphere of the room is largely created by the light from the window that in turn gives form to the very plain walls. This interior is the creation of Ray Whitledge Miniatures.

A HOUSE FOR
ALL SEASONS

When creating the interior of a dollhouse, it is a good idea to have a unifying theme, which, when the house is viewed as a whole, gives a pleasing coordination between the rooms. Each of the four rooms of this "house for all seasons" is decorated in accordance with one of the seasons. The subtle themes of spring, summer, fall, and winter work together to create an overall consistency of approach.

▲ In the family room, the theme is winter where the imaginary owners display a collection of Christmas items. The plaid patterned carpet, now associated with this time of year, and the container of holly with berries and a poinsettia plant all add to the theme.

◄ The bedroom is decorated in the colors of spring. The theme is echoed by the use of outdoor furniture inside, bright yellow flowers, and a pair of white doves.

▼ The summertime kitchen is decorated with the colors of sky, sea, and sun, with plants and flowers in full bloom. The floral light fixture, beehive honeypot, and buckets and spade are effective touches that enliven the whole.

▲ Fall colors predominate in the living room, which has soft green leaves as a recurring theme. The wallpaper panels are available already printed. The furniture and accessories have been gilded to give an original touch.

RURAL IDYLLS

In a dollhouse setting, as in the real world, you can create charming interiors with old-style furnishings and decoration, but if you want to maintain a contemporary country look, don't forget to add a few modern touches.

▼ French cafe-style furniture sets the scene for this room. While the cooking range provides a traditional touch, the modern kitchen cabinets in natural wood house up-to-date appliances to emphasize that this is a contemporary room.

▲ This is an English farmhouse kitchen built for the 1990s. It contains a miniature coal-fired cooking range, an old-fashioned butler's sink, and scrubbed pine kitchen table with matching chairs. The pretty patterned wallpaper and vegetable print curtains complete the country look.

▲ The background for this
setting by Sue Peel
Miniatures is meant to look old,
although the scene is modern.
The charm of this interior lies in
its timeless quality.

DESIGNER INTERIORS

Professionally designed and
carefully structured interiors
are a feature of many homes
today. These three miniature
interiors are the work of Ray
Whitledge, an interior designer
who had considerable
experience in designing full-size
homes before starting to work
in miniature.

▼ | "Morning Splendour" is the
title of this glorious interior.
Light from behind is used to
dramatic effect. The classical
forms in the Chippendale-style
chairs skillfully coordinates with
more modern pieces to create a
glamorous look for the 1990s.

▲ | This elegant lobby entitled
"A Gentleman's Haven" is
carefully coordinated in somber
masculine mood. Note the
interesting decorative treatment
of the woodwork and columns.

▲ Classical forms used in
conjunction with modern
wall coverings and fabrics
combine to create a harmonious
result. In miniature, as in
real life, a room built around
favorite pieces of any style can
produce a room of contemporary
eclectic look.

PRESENT DAY INTERIORS

Most of us live our lives surrounded by things connected to both past and present, and our homes portray this electic mix. Nevertheless scenes can be created that represent aspects of life solely in the style of the present day.

▼ There can be no doubt that this hot tub and sun deck setting belong to the late 20th century and in future years will undoubtedly prove most amusing. Note the styling of the aviator sunglasses, tennis racket, and boom box ghetto blaster which already seem a little out of date.

▲ Although motorbikes have
been around for nearly all
this century these two are
obviously current models.
Set in a simple box this
motorbike repair shop was
made as a present for a biker
enthusiast, and clearly reflects
his special interest.

SOUVENIR HOMES

Memories of travel or excursions outside the home can be reproduced in miniature, forming a souvenir of your trip. Pieces collected on vacation and utilized in a room set can create an interior with special resonances.

▲ An exotic safari might have been the inspiration for this escapist home. The atmospheric details include a mosquito net, tiger-skin rugs, and even a parrot.

▲ | A visit to Santa Barbara, California, inspired this little scene, which incorporates both the Spanish-style influence of the area as well as some of the inhabitants.

▶ | This shady little courtyard has been created in the style of the Southwestern states, complete with adobe rooms and appropriate furnishings and accessories. The up-to-date figures will probably look quite curious at some time in the future.

SPECIAL COLLECTIONS

Many of us admire objects that we are never likely to be in a position to collect full size. However, many of these objects are available in scaled-down form. A collection of such objects carefully arranged can create a very special scene.

▼ This museum basement room was created to house odd categories of miniatures left over from other projects. Together they give the impression of waiting to be placed in the specialist displays in the museum upstairs.

▶ A scale model windowsill was created for a collection of miniature blue glass. This inventive device proved to be an effective way of displaying the collection. Placed in a real window facing the sun, the arrangement is illuminated from behind by natural daylight.

▼ This Christmas store was made with the idea of collecting in mind, and the pieces were added over a period of time. Once the wallpaper was hung and basic shop fixtures painted a seasonal green, items of merchandise could be put in position as they were acquired.

▲ A collection of miniature folk art formed a display in this country gift shop. Other items have been placed on shelves. After the nucleus of a collection has been assembled, the creation of a store provides a wonderful excuse for buying more pieces.

Index

Credits

Quarto would like to thank the following for supplying photographs and for permission to reproduce copyright material. While every effort has been made to acknowledge copyright holders we would like to apologize should there have been any omissions.

KEY – T = top   B = below   C = center   L = left   R = right

Dijon Ltd *p.8*; The Dollshouse Toys Ltd *p.131*(L); The Doll House Museum *p.135*; Nick Forder *p.1, 2, 11*(T, L), *72, 108, 110, 111, 114*(R), *115, 116, 117, 118, 119, 120, 121, 122, 123, 126, 128, 129, 134, 136, 137, 138, 139, 140*(T), *142, 143, 144, 145, 146, 147, 148, 149, 150, 151, 152, 153, 154, 155, 156, 157*; Hever Castle *141*(C); Honeychurch Toys Ltd *p.10, 126*(BL), *130*(L); Carole and Barry Kaye Museum of Miniatures *p.112, 113, 114*(L); Peter Mattinson *p.78, 98, 131*(R); Mini Mundus *p.11*(BL), *22, 124, 125, 130*(R); Toy and Miniature Museum of Kansas City *p.132, 133*.